UPGRADING AND REPAIRING PCS
BUILD A PC WITH SCOTT MUELLER

D0001578

Scott Mueller

800 East 96th Street,
Indianapolis, Indiana 46240

Build a PC with Scott Mueller

Many of the designations used by manufacturers and sellers to distinguish their products are claimed as trademarks. Where those designations appear in this book, and the publisher was aware of a trademark claim, the designations have been printed with initial capital letters or in all capitals.

The authors and publisher have taken care in the preparation of this book and DVD, but make no expressed or implied warranty of any kind and assume no responsibility for errors or omissions. No liability is assumed for incidental or consequential damages in connection with or arising out of the use of the information or programs contained herein.

The publisher offers excellent discounts on this product when ordered in quantity for bulk purchases or special sales, which may include electronic versions and/or custom covers and content particular to your business, training goals, marketing focus, and branding interests. For more information, please contact:

U.S. Corporate and Government Sales
(800) 382-3419
corpsales@pearsontechgroup.com

For sales outside the United States please contact:

International Sales
international@pearsoned.com
Visit us on the Web: http://www.quepublishing.com

Library of Congress Cataloging-in-Publication Data:

ISBN-13: 978-0-789-73775-5

ISBN-10: 0-7897-3775-2

Second printing: December 2009

Copyright © 2008 by Que Publishing

All rights reserved. Printed in the United States of America. This publication is protected by copyright, and permission must be obtained from the publisher prior to any prohibited reproduction, storage in a retrieval system, or transmission in any form or by any means, electronic, mechanical, photocopying, recording, or likewise. For information regarding permissions, write to:

Pearson Education, Inc.
Rights and Contracts Department
75 Arlington Street, Suite 300
Boston, MA 02116
Fax: (617) 848-7047

This material may be distributed only subject to the terms and conditions set forth in the Open Publication License, v1.0 or later (the latest version is presently available at http://www.opencontent.org/openpub/).

Associate Publisher
Greg Wiegand

Acquisitions Editor
Rick Kughen

Development Editor
Rick Kughen

DVD Developer
Lynn Mueller

Managing Editor
Patrick Kanouse

Project Editor
Jennifer Gallant

Copy Editor
Keith Cline

Technical Editor
Mark Reddin

Publishing Coordinator
Cindy Teeters

Interior Designer
Anne Jones

Cover Designer
Anne Jones

Composition
Mark Shirar

Contents

About the Author

Scott Mueller is president of Mueller Technical Research (MTR), an international research and corporate training firm. Since 1982, MTR has produced the industry's most in-depth, accurate, and effective seminars, books, articles, videos, and FAQs covering PC hardware and data recovery. MTR maintains a client list that includes Fortune 500 companies, the U.S. and foreign governments, major software and hardware corporations, and PC enthusiasts and entrepreneurs. His seminars have been presented to several thousands of PC support professionals throughout the world.

Scott personally teaches seminars nationwide covering all aspects of PC hardware (including troubleshooting, maintenance, repair, and upgrade), A+ Certification, and data recovery/forensics. He has a knack for making technical topics not only understandable, but entertaining as well; his classes are never boring! If you have 10 or more people to train, Scott can design and present a custom seminar for your organization.

Although he has taught classes nearly nonstop since 1982, Scott is best known as the author of the longest running, most popular, and most comprehensive PC hardware book in the world, *Upgrading and Repairing PCs*, which has not only been produced in more than 18 editions, but has also become the core of an entire series of books.

Scott has authored many books over the past 20+ years, including *Upgrading and Repairing PCs* (1st through 18th and Academic editions); *Upgrading and Repairing Laptops* (1st and 2nd editions); *Upgrading and Repairing Windows*; *Upgrading and Repairing PCs: A+ Certification Study Guide* (1st and 2nd editions); *Upgrading and Repairing PCs Technician's Portable Reference* (1st and 2nd editions); *Upgrading and Repairing PCs Field Guide*; *Upgrading and Repairing PCs Quick Reference*; *Upgrading and Repairing PCs, Linux Edition*; *Killer PC Utilities*; *The IBM PS/2 Handbook*; and *Que's Guide to Data Recovery*.

Scott has produced several video training packages covering PC hardware, including a six-hour, CD-based seminar titled Upgrading and Repairing PCs Training Course: A Digital Seminar from Scott Mueller. Scott has also produced other videos over the years, including *Upgrading and Repairing PCs Video* (12th edition); *Your PC: The Inside Story*; as well as 2+ hours of free video training that were included in each of the 10th and 12th through 18th editions of *Upgrading and Repairing PCs* and in several editions of *Upgrading and Repairing Laptops* and *Upgrading and Repairing Windows*.

Contact MTR directly if you have a unique book, article, or video project in mind, or if you want Scott to conduct a custom PC troubleshooting, repair, maintenance, upgrade, or data-recovery seminar tailored for your organization:

Mueller Technical Research
3700 Grayhawk Drive
Algonquin, IL 60102-6325
(847) 854-6794
(847) 854-6795 Fax
Internet: scottmueller@compuserve.com
Web: http://www.upgradingandrepairingpcs.com
        http://www.scottmueller.com

Scott has a private forum exclusively for those who have purchased one of his recent books or DVDs. Visit http://forum.scottmueller.com to view the forum. Note that posting is only available to registered members.

Scott's premiere work, *Upgrading and Repairing PCs*, has sold well over 2 million copies, making it by far the most popular and longest-running PC hardware book on the market today. Scott has been featured in *Forbes* magazine and has written several articles for *PC World* magazine, *Maximum PC* magazine, the Scott Mueller Forum, various computer and automotive newsletters, and the *Upgrading and Repairing PCs* website.

If you have suggestions for the next version of this book, any comments about the book in general, or new book or article topics you would like to see covered, send them to Scott via email at scottmueller@compuserve.com.

When he is not working on PC-related books or on the road teaching seminars, Scott can usually be found in the garage working on anything with wheels and an engine.

Dedication

To my friend Mike - Hey..., hey, wake up!

Acknowledgments

I would like to thank my wife Lynn for doing the filming, DVD editing, and production. She is essential to all of my video projects. I'd also like to thank my friend Mike Sundstrom, who helped film some of the segments and who helped tremendously by acquiring all of the items used in the shoot. Finally, I'd like to thank all of the people at Que for helping to make these videos possible. A special thanks goes to Rick Kughen, who is the Editor-in-Chief on all of my projects.

We Want to Hear from You!

As the reader of this book, *you* are our most important critic and commentator. We value your opinion and want to know what we're doing right, what we could do better, what areas you'd like to see us publish in, and any other words of wisdom you're willing to pass our way.

As an associate publisher for Que Publishing, I welcome your comments. You can email or write me directly to let me know what you did or didn't like about this book—as well as what we can do to make our books better.

Please note that I cannot help you with technical problems related to the topic of this book. We do have a User Services group, however, where I will forward specific technical questions related to the book to the appropriate parties.

When you write, please be sure to include this book's title and author as well as your name, email address, and phone number. I will carefully review your comments and share them with the author and editors who worked on the book.

Email: feedback@quepublishing.com

Mail: Greg Wiegand
         Associate Publisher
         Que Publishing
         800 East 96th Street
         Indianapolis, IN 46240 USA

Reader Services

Visit our website and register this book at http://www.quepublishing.com/register for convenient access to any updates, downloads, or errata that might be available for this book.

Upgrading and Repairing: Build a PC with Scott Mueller

Welcome to *Upgrading and Repairing: Build a PC with Scott Mueller*. In this video, and in the included booklet, I cover all aspects of building a PC from scratch, including everything from the initial component selection, to actually building the system and getting it running. The booklet you are reading now is designed to enhance the video, adding important details and reference information to aid in the process.

Video Segment 1: Goals When Building a PC

One of the best features of PCs is their nearly infinite variability. There are so many different components to choose from, and they can be both configured and assembled in any number of ways. As with many things, you must consider a number of trade-offs when building a PC from scratch. For example, if performance is the ultimate goal and cost is no consideration, the type of PC you could build is entirely different from one where a more limited budget is in effect. Although no single set of choices results in one perfect PC for everybody, it is certainly possible to come up with a reasonable set of goals to achieve.

I've built hundreds of PCs over the more than 25 years I've been in the business, and with the exception of systems for specialized purposes such as servers, database processors, or even pure gaming systems, my usual goals in building a universally useful PC are the same. I want the resulting system to be

- Fast
- Inexpensive
- Upgradeable
- Practical and reliable

Note

Note that the specific choices in components that I show and use in this system are not important, because those will change over time. As new or different components are introduced, my choices will change based on what components are available, what they cost, and who or what the specific system is being designed for. With that in mind, I try to focus more on general principles rather than specific components.

Fast

For the system to be fast, I recommend the system include the following components/considerations:

- **Dual- or quad-core processor**—The days of multicore computing are here, and because of the relative low cost and yet high performance of multicore processors, I don't recommend single-core processors for all but the most economical or low-power designs.

- **Dual-channel RAM**—There are relatively few differences in performance between different types of memory such as DDR2 or DDR3, or with different speeds within a type such as 667MHz or 800MHz DDR2. But one feature that makes a larger difference is running memory in dual channel (also called *interleaved*) mode versus single-channel or noninterleaved mode. By installing memory modules in matched pairs, with one of each module in a different channel, modern motherboards will run them in dual-channel mode, resulting in twice the memory bandwidth. Although this will not have nearly as large an effect on overall system performance, it is the easiest and most economical way to optimize memory performance.

- **Gigabit Ethernet**—Many people or families today have a growing collection of digital data to deal with, including videos, photos, music files, documents, and more. With sharing or even backing up these files over a network becoming commonplace, as well as the larger number and sizes of the files accumulating on systems, using Gigabit Ethernet can increase network performance up to 10 times that of the slower 100Mb speed. With Gigabit Ethernet adapters available for $10 or less (and some even built in to the motherboard) and the availability of low-cost gigabit switches (used to interconnect the devices on the network), there is little excuse for not running your network at gigabit speeds. When building a PC, choose a motherboard that incorporates Gigabit Ethernet built in; or if the built-in port only runs 100Mb, add a Gigabit Ethernet card (you might need to disable the on-board network adapter through the BIOS; check your motherboard manual for details).

- **eSATA external drive backup**—USB and FireWire are adequate for connecting external backup drives, but by choosing a motherboard with eSATA (external Serial ATA) support built in, you can effectively double the speed of your backups.

- **Optional: RAID 0 (striped) boot partition**—With hard drives becoming cheaper all the time, and modern motherboards available with integrated chipset-based RAID controllers offering performance not previously available with card-based RAID implementations, I recommend considering the use of a RAID 0 boot volume. Because RAID 0 more than doubles the chance for failure, data should still be stored on either a standalone data drive or RAID 1 (mirrored) volume. However, for booting the OS, maximizing the OS page-file performance, and loading drivers and applications, RAID 0 offers at least double the performance of a standalone drive. There is some risk because if any drive in a RAID 0 volume fails, all files on the volume will be lost; but because the OS, drivers, and applications can easily be backed up and reloaded, the risk may be warranted given the performance gains. Although running a RAID 0 boot volume might not be for everybody, it can dramatically increase the performance of the system as a whole.

Inexpensive

PCs have always offered excellent value, especially when compared to less-popular alternative types of personal computers, but you can build a PC to fit in many different price ranges. For most uses, you can easily keep the total cost of a system to $1,000 or less, and a relatively high-performance full-featured system can easily be built in the $2,000 or less range.

Starter System with Upgrade Potential

For a general-use PC, I like to keep the cost as low as possible, while still allowing for performance and future upgrades. For me this means building a system with as many integrated components as possible, while also containing the necessary slots or ports where future upgrades can be added. I recommend purchasing a motherboard that includes at least the following integrated components:

- Gigabit Ethernet
- HD (high-definition) audio
- USB/FireWire/eSATA

Other integrated components that might be considered include the following:

- Video
- RAID (chipset based)

Of those, integrated video is perhaps the most controversial, because there seems to be a relatively large gap in performance between integrated video and the video you find on available add-in cards. If you are building a system where gaming is important, you will almost definitely want an add-in video card. In that case, you might want to choose a motherboard without integrated video, because you will be installing a video card anyway, which will automatically disable the integrated video.

But even so, I usually find that having the integrated video option adds no cost to the motherboard, and motherboards with integrated video still normally have an expansion slot allowing a video card to be installed initially or as an upgrade later. This means that if you have a video card installed you essentially have a backup video adapter in the system for free. I find the integrated video especially useful when troubleshooting or initially configuring a system. And especially I find that when a system is a few years old, I usually like to rebuild it as a server or media player, and having the ability to revert back to the integrated video is a great feature.

If you are considering the use of RAID, having chipset-based RAID integrated into your motherboard is something you should consider. Except for high-availability servers where RAID 6 is desired, chipset-based RAID will normally outperform that of any card-based RAID solutions.

One or Two Internal Hard Disk Drives

For the lowest cost, you should build your system with a single internal hard drive. If desired, it can be partitioned into multiple partitions, say one for boot (OS/drivers/applications) and one for data; but in most cases, I recommend leaving the drive as a single partition and organizing your data into a folder rather than a separate partition.

Another option is to use two drives, one for booting the system and the other for data. With two drives and an integrated RAID controller, you have the option of even higher performance or reliability, or both. You can run both drives in a RAID 0 (striped) configuration for double the performance (and unfortunately half the reliability), or in a RAID 1 configuration for the same performance as a single drive (or slightly better in the case of Intel's chipset-based RAID, which does load balancing) and double the reliability.

Intel's so-called Matrix RAID also offers a third choice—running both RAID 0 and RAID 1 volumes on the same two drives. Note that I am not recommending this setup for everybody, but it does allow the best of both RAID 0 and RAID 1 on two drives. If you are willing to spend more on four drives, I recommend a RAID 10 setup, which combines striping and mirroring in an array with the best of both features.

Upgradeable

One of the best features of self-built PCs is their inherent upgradeability. But with a careful selection of components, you can improve on the future upgradeability of a system over what it might be otherwise. For example, choosing a motherboard with one chipset over another might allow a wider range of future processors/memory to be installed.

- **Intel-based systems**—If you are building an Intel processor–based system, I recommend choosing a motherboard based on the Intel 3x series chipsets over the older 9xx series chipsets. The 3x series supports the newer Penryn-based Wolfdale (dual-core) and Yorkfield (quad-core) processors built on 45nm (nanometer) technology. This means that even if you install a current 65nm Conroe (dual-core) or Kentsfield (quad-core) Core2 processor, you can later upgrade to the newer 45nm processors without having to change the motherboard/memory in the process. In addition, the 3x series chipsets also have the following capabilities:

- Up to 1333MHz Front Side Bus (FSB)
- Up to 8GB RAM
- PCIe 2.0 (X38)
- Crossfire (X38)
- Optional DDR3 memory (X38, P35, G33, G35)

Those chipsets that support DDR3 also support DDR2, but not on the same motherboard. That means that the motherboard you choose will be designed to support either DDR2 or DDR3, but not both.

- **AMD-based systems**—If you are building an AMD processor–based system, for maximum upgradeability make sure you choose a chipset that supports the newer AMD Phenom X2 and X4 processors. Motherboards with these chipsets also support either Socket AM2+ and DDR2 memory or Socket AM3 and DDR3 memory.

Industry-Standard Form Factors

An important consideration for future upgradeability is the choice of motherboard, chassis, and power-supply form factors. For maximum future upgradeability, you can choose an ATX chassis, which will support both ATX and microATX motherboards (and ATX power supplies). You can also go with a smaller microATX chassis, but in that case I generally recommend those that still use standard ATX power supplies, too. You can get small form factor (SFF) chassis that support microATX motherboards, but those often use smaller, less-powerful, and less-available power-supply form factors.

PCIe x16 Slot for Video

If you are choosing a motherboard with integrated video, make sure it still has a PCIe x16 slot allowing you to add a video card later. For example, you might want to add a video card later if you start gaming and find that the performance of the integrated video just doesn't cut it. If you want to enable the ultimate gaming experience now or in the future, choose a board with dual PCIe x16 slots supporting either Crossfire (ATI) or SLI (NVIDIA) dual graphics card solutions.

Chassis Bays for Additional Drives

Another factor in the choice of your chassis is the number of different drive bays that are available. Modern chassis will generally have three types of drive bays:

- **5.25" external**—The 5.25" external bays are primarily designed for optical (CD/DVD) drives, but they can also hold 3.5" hard disk drives using simple adapter brackets. Another option for those bays are external port adapters, fan controllers, or even storage drawers.

- **3.5" external**—The 3.5" external bays are primarily designed for floppy drives, but they can also hold front-panel port adapters or fan controllers. In some cases, it is possible to also mount a hard drive in these bays, but that might require minor modifications in some chassis.

- **3.5" internal**—Finally, the internal 3.5" bays are designed for hard disk drives. In general, you want to ensure that there are enough of these bays to hold all the internal hard disks you want to install. If the chassis supports more than two drives, I highly recommend ensuring that provisions are available to install a fan to cool the drives. In most cases, you will find a position for one or more optional front-mounted fans that are designed to blow air directly on the installed internal 3.5" drives.

RAID Ready

By choosing a motherboard that has built-in chipset-based RAID, and by enabling the RAID controller before the initial OS installation (even if you are only installing a single drive in a non-RAID configuration), you will make the system what we call *RAID ready*. Being RAID ready means that the system can easily be upgraded from non-RAID to a RAID configuration at any time in the future, without having to reinstall the OS or restore any files. You could, for example, add one or more additional drives in the future, and then perform what is called a *RAID migration*, which moves the volume and all of its contents from the single drive to the multiple-drive RAID volume, without reinstalling anything. Even more amazing is that the system can even be used normally while the migration is taking place.

Future CPU Overclock/Upgrade Possible

By carefully choosing your motherboard, processor, and RAM, you can build a system that will be overclockable. For example, because the different speed-grade processors in a given family are built on the same die, in general the slower the rated speed grade of the processor you purchase, the more you will be able to overclock it in the future. As a specific example, the Intel Core2 Quad Q6600 is rated at the relatively slow speed of 2.4GHz, yet many people have success in overclocking it to 3GHz and beyond. That is a 25% or greater increase in speed, for little or no cost.

The most important issue with overclocking is the choice of motherboard. Most motherboards installed in store-bought systems don't allow overclocking for obvious warranty and support reasons, nor do most of the Intel desktop motherboards. On the other hand, the Intel "extreme series" motherboards do allow overclocking, as do most non-Intel boards such as those from Abit, Asus, Gigabyte, MSI, and so on.

In addition to the motherboard, overclocking is obviously influenced by the capabilities of your processor, and also involves the memory. There are some risks with overclocking, but if that is something you want to try, choose your motherboard, processor, and even your memory with overclocking in mind.

Caution

When building a system for a friend, relative, customer, or client where you will be the one providing support, you might want to avoid overclocking because of the potential for additional instability or problems.

Practical and Reliable

Few people will tolerate a system that locks up all the time, or one that is extremely loud. The overall size and shape of the system might be important, too. For example, you probably don't want a full-size ATX tower system as a media center PC in your living room. Try to consider what the final use of the system will be, where it will be installed, and what you will be using it for.

Standard MicroATX Form Factor Motherboard and Chassis

Although full-size ATX motherboads and chassis offer the ultimate in expandability and upgrade-ability, I often don't need or want a system that large. With most important features integrated into the motherboard already, additional card slots often go unused. The same goes for additional drive bays. Having four external 5.25" drive bays makes little sense if you are only going to install a single optical drive. I find that for most normal uses, a smaller form factor microATX chassis and motherboard is more appropriate than the full-size alternatives.

Processor and Chipset from the Same Manufacturer

In general, I have found greater reliability and system integrity when mating processors and chipsets from the same manufacturer. What this means in essence is that if I am building a system with an Intel processor, I generally like to use a motherboard with an Intel chipset, and when building a motherboard with an AMD processor, I like to use a motherboard with an AMD chipset.

RAID 1 (Mirrored) Data Partition

If stability and integrity is valued over performance, you might consider installing two drives and just running them in a straight RAID 1 (mirrored) setup. This will provide redundancy, in that if one drive fails you will not lose any data and the system will remain running. You can then replace the drive and rebuild the array while still using the system.

Caution

If any drive in a RAID 0 array fails, the entire array will be unavailable and all data will be lost. If you use a RAID 0 setup, performing regular backups to a separate external drive is not only a good idea, it's *crucial*.

External eSATA/USB Backup Drive

Backup is an important part of system reliability and integrity, and unfortunately many people fail to consider backup when building a PC. If the PC is part of a home or small office network, you can use a server or network-attached storage device for backup, but the simplest and fastest form of backup is to use an external drive directly attached to the system. Interface choices for external drives are normally USB, FireWire, and more recently eSATA. Of those, eSATA offers relatively double the performance of the others, which can cut backup times in half.

Quiet Fans

Noise (or the lack thereof) is an important consideration for system practicality. A user of a full-bore gaming system might be willing to tolerate the additional noise of dual fan-cooled video cards and exotic gamer cases with numerous fans, but many people prefer a quieter system. It is possible to cut the noise in a system by choosing quieter fans, hard drives, and other components. If a quiet system is the goal, look for lower-speed fans and those with fluid bearings (and hard drives with fluid bearings). Also note that larger fans spin more slowly and generate less heat and noise while moving more air through your system.

Video Segment 2: Selecting Components

In this segment, I show all the components necessary to build a system and provide additional detail on all of them.

Motherboard

If the CPU is the brain of the system, the chipset is the central nervous system, connecting the brain to all the other components and peripherals. Because of the relative importance of the chipset to everything else, when choosing the components for a system, I usually start with the chipset, and often spend more time deciding on what chipset I will use than I do on any other component in the system. The chipset will govern the type/range of processors that will be supported, and the types of buses, memory sockets, integrated components such as video, audio, and RAID, and so on. Because so many other things depend on the chipset, I recommend making that selection carefully.

For the purposes of this video, originally I intended to build an Intel system using a Core2 Quad processor, with either older 9xx or newer 3x chipsets. However, for maximum future upgradeability, I ultimately chose to go with a 3x chipset motherboard. The current 3x series chipsets include the following:

- X38 for high-performance systems
    - 1333/1066/800MHz FSB
    - No built-in video
    - Two PCI x16 slots (Crossfire support)
    - 8GB max. DDR2 or DDR3 up to 1333MHz
    - 6 SATA
    - Most likely full ATX

- P35 for medium to high performance
    - 1333/1066/800MHz FSB
    - No built-in video
    - One PCI x16 slot
    - 8GB max. DDR2 or DDR3 up to 1066MHz
    - 4-6 SATA
    - Most likely full ATX

- G33/G35 for medium to high performance

  - 1333/1066/800MHz FSB

  - Built-in video

  - One PCI x16 slot

  - 8GB max. DDR2 or DDR3 up to 1066MHz

  - 4-6 SATA

  - Most likely microATX

- P31/G31 for low-performance entry-level systems

  - 4GB max. DDR2

Wanting the most features in a microATX form factor along with integrated video, I settled on the G33 chipset as my choice. I could have also chosen the X38 for a maximum-performance system, but that would most likely come on a full-size ATX motherboard and lack integrated video.

Several motherboards meet those criteria, including the following:

> Foxconn G33M-S:
> http://www.newegg.com/Product/Product.aspx?Item=N82E16813186123
>
> GIGABYTE GA-G33M-DS2R:
> http://www.newegg.com/Product/Product.aspx?Item=N82E16813128053
>
> Intel DG33TL: http://www.newegg.com/Product/Product.aspx?Item=N82E16813121315
>
> MSI G33M-FI: http://www.newegg.com/Product/Product.aspx?Item=N82E16813130120

Important features found in most of these boards include the following:

- Integrated video with single- or dual-display support

- 1 PCIe x16 slot for a video upgrade

- 1 or 2 PCIe x1 slots

- 1 or 2 PCI slots

- 6 SATA ports with 1 or 2 eSATA

- 1 PATA port supporting up to 2 PATA drives

- Gigabit Ethernet

- 12 USB ports

- 2x 1394 (FireWire) ports

- HD (high-definition) audio

- RAID 0, 1, 5, and 10 support with up to 6 drives per array

Although these boards have most of the same features, there are a few minor differences between them. For example, the Intel DG33TL does not offer any overclocking settings in the BIOS setup, and lacks legacy ports such as a floppy controller and PS/2 keyboard/mouse ports. If those features are important, I recommend you skip that board and choose one of the others. One unique feature of the Intel board is built-in support for dual video displays without adding any other hardware, including both VGA and DVI-D connectors.

For motherboards lacking legacy PS/2 connectors, you can of course use only USB keyboards and mice, or attach older PS/2 keyboards and mice using an adapter such as one of the following:

> SYBA SD-PCI-UPS2 USB to Dual PS2 case mounted adapter:
> http://www.newegg.com/Product/Product.aspx?Item=N82E16815124046
>
> BYTECC BT-2000 USB to Dual PS2 Adapter:
> http://www.newegg.com/Product/Product.aspx?Item=N82E16812101117

CPU

For the processor, I want to use one of the Core2 Quad processors, the most economical of which is the Core2 Quad Q6600. This processor has the following features:

- Core2 Quad Q6600
- 2.4GHz rated speed
- 1066MHz FSB
- 8MB L2 cache
- Kentsfield core
- Socket LGA775
- 65nm technology
- 0.85V–1.5V core voltage
- 32/64-bit (EM64T) operation
- Hardware virtualization (Virtual PC/VMware)
- EIST (Enhanced Intel Speedstep Technology)
- Execute Disable (XD) bit

You can look up more information on any Intel processor if you know the sSpec (specification) number and enter it at the Intel Processor Spec Finder site: http://processorfinder.intel.com.

You can also see what different processors of a given type are available at that site if you browse by the processor family. Looking up the Core2 Quad for example, you'll see that there are actually two different versions (steppings) of the Q6600 processor, each with different sSpec (specification) numbers. A processor stepping is a version of a given processor, with later steppings generally indicating newer and better versions of the same chip. When given a choice between different steppings, you'll usually find that the later one has some improvements. Looking at the two different Q6600 processors that are listed, you can see the following differences:

- SL9UM sSpec number
  - B3 core stepping

- 06F7h CPUID string

- 105W Thermal Design Power (PCG 05B)

- 62.2°C (144°F) thermal specification

- SLACR sSpec number

  - G0 core stepping

  - 06FBh CPUID string

  - 95W Thermal Design Power (PCG 05A)

  - 71°C (160°F) thermal specification

As you can see, the later stepping uses less power and runs cooler (95W TDP vs. 105W TDP), and also has a higher temperature tolerance (160°F vs. 144°F). The PCG (Platform Compatibility Guide) is directly related to the maximum amount of power the processor can use, which is called the Thermal Design Power (TDP).

But how do you tell exactly which processor is which? There are several ways. If the processor is installed in a system, you can use software to read out the CPUID and internal stepping codes. A popular program for this purpose is the free CPU-Z program available from http://www.cpuid.com.

Figure 1 shows the CPU-Z output for the Core2 Quad Q6600 in the system I built in the video.

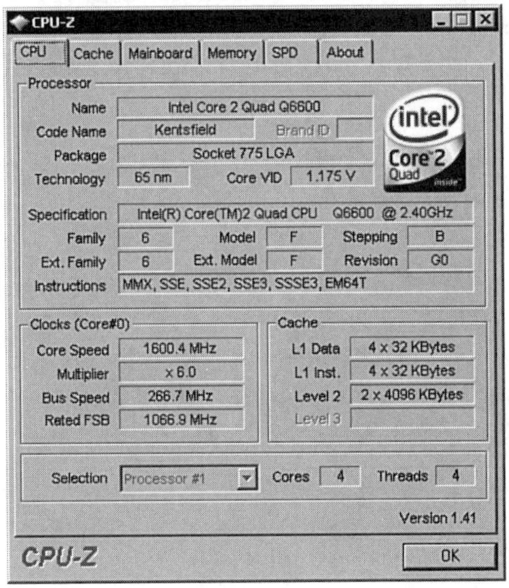

Figure 1   CPU-Z processor information display.

Note the Family, Model, and Stepping information, which corresponds to the CPUID of 06FBh (the *h* indicates this is a hexadecimal number) for this processor, which corresponds to an sSpec of SLACR (a very overclockable CPU). Also you can see the revision is listed as G0, which also corresponds to the stepping as Intel reports for the SLACR sStep version.

This is very useful if you want to identify a processor that is already installed, but it might be even more useful to know what processor is in the box *before* you install it, or better yet, before you even *buy* it. The sSpec number for a given processor is laser etched directly onto the heat spreader (metal plate covering the top of the chip), and is also printed on the label on the side of the box. Although you cannot see the markings on the chip once it is installed, you can see the label on the box even before it is opened. Figure 2 shows the label on the boxed processor.

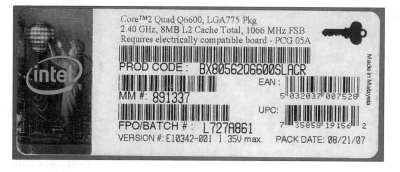

Figure 2   Boxed processor label.

The sSpec number is the last five characters in the product code. For example, if the product code shown on the label is BX80562Q6600SLACR, the sSpec for the processor in the box is SLACR.

If you have a raw (unboxed) processor that is not installed in a system, you can read the laser etching on the chip to determine the sSpec number. Figure 3 shows a magnified picture of the laser etch marks on a processor. This particular example shows a Pentium D 830 with an sSpec number of SL88S.

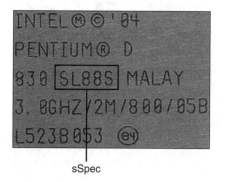

sSpec

Figure 3   Laser etch marks on a processor heat spreader.

Once you know the sSpec of any processor, you can use the Intel Processor Spec Finder page (http://processorfinder.intel.com) to determine all the important specifications for that processor.

Platform Compatibility Guide

Another specification reported for Intel processors is what Intel calls the Platform Compatibility Guide (PCG). This directly relates to the maximum power the processor will use, and is designed to ensure that the motherboard and chassis you select are up to the task of powering and cooling the processor.

Modern processors are powered via a 4- or 8-pin +12V cable connected between the power supply and the motherboard. Modern motherboards are designed to support a wide range of different processors. However, because processor power consumption has increased, especially for high-end chips, the voltage regulator circuitry on a given motherboard might not have been designed to supply sufficient power to support all processors that might otherwise fit in the processor socket. To help eliminate the potential power problems that could result (including intermittent lockups or even damage such as damaged components or burned circuits), Intel created a power standard called the Platform Compatibility Guide. The PCG is marked on Intel boxed (retail) processors and motherboards. It is designed for system builders to use it as an easy way to know the power requirements of a processor and to ensure that the motherboard can meet those requirements.

The PCG is designated as a two- or three-digit alphanumeric value (for example, 05A), where the first two digits represent the year the particular specification was introduced and the optional third character stands for the market segment. PCG designations where the third character is *A* apply to processors and motherboards that fall in the low-end market (requiring less power), whereas designations where the third character is *B* apply to processors and motherboards that fall in the high-end market (requiring more power). Motherboards that support high-end processors by default also support low-end processors, but not the other way around. For example, you can install a processor with a PCG specification of 05A in a motherboard with a PCG specification of 05B, but if you install a 05B processor in a motherboard rated 05A, power problems will result. In other words, you can always install a processor with lower power requirements in a higher-power-capable motherboard, but not the other way around.

Although the PCG figures were specifically intended to apply to the processor and motherboard, they can also be used to specify minimum power-supply requirements. Table 1 shows the PCG numbers and the power recommendations they prescribe.

Table 1   Intel Platform Compatibility Guide (PCG) +12V Connector Power Recommendations

PCG Number	Year Introduced	Market Segment	CPU Power Specification	Continuous +12V Rating	Peak +12V Rating
06	2006	All	65W	8 A	13 A
04A	2004	Low end	84W	13 A	16.5 A
05A	2005	Low end	95W	13 A	16.5 A
04B	2004	High end	115W	13 A	16.5 A
05B	2005	High end	130W	16 A	19 A

The power supply should be able to supply peak current for at least 10ms.

Choosing a power supply with the required minimum output on the +12V connector helps to ensure proper operation of the system.

Memory

Depending on which chipset/motherboard you select, any system you build today will use either DDR2 or DDR3 SDRAM (synchronous dynamic random access memory). The DDR designation stands for double data rate, which indicates that these types of memory transfer twice per clock cycle, or double the rate of older SDRAM.

DDR2 Synchronous Dynamic Random Access Memory

DDR2 is just a faster version of DDR memory: It achieves higher throughput by using differential pairs of signal wires to allow faster signaling without noise and interference problems. DDR2 is still double data rate just as with DDR, but the modified signaling method enables higher clock speeds to be achieved with more immunity to noise and cross-talk between the signals. The additional signals required for differential pairs add to the pin count—DDR2 dual inline memory modules (DIMMs) have 240 pins, which is more than the 184 pins found on DDR DIMMs. The original DDR specification officially topped out at 400MHz (although faster unofficial over-clocked modules were produced), whereas DDR2 starts at 400MHz and goes up to an official maximum of 1066MHz. Table 2 shows the various official Joint Electron Device Engineering Council (JEDEC)-approved DDR2 module types and bandwidth specifications.

Table 2   JEDEC Standard DDR2 Module (240-Pin DIMM) Speeds and Transfer Rates

Module Standard	Chip Type	Clock Speed (MHz)	Cycles per Clock	Bus Speed (MTps)	Bus Width (Bytes)	Transfer Rate (MBps)	Dual-Channel Transfer Rate (MBps)
PC2-3200	DDR2-400	200	2	400	8	3200	6,400
PC2-4200	DDR2-533	266	2	533	8	4266	8,533
PC2-5300	DDR2-667	333	2	667	8	5333	10,667
PC2-6400	DDR2-800	400	2	800	8	6400	12,800
PC2-8500	DDR2-1066	533	2	1066	8	8533	17,066

MTps = Megatransfers per second

MBps = Megabytes per second

DIMM = Dual inline memory module

DDR = Double data rate

The fastest official JEDEC-approved standard is DDR2-1066, which are chips that run at an effective speed of 1066MHz (really megatransfers per second), resulting in modules designated PC2-8500 having a bandwidth of 8533MBps. However, just as with DDR, many of the module manufacturers produce even faster modules designed for overclocked systems. These are sold as modules with unofficial designations and performance figures that exceed the standard ratings.

Table 3 shows the popular unofficial speed ratings I've seen on the market. Note that because the speeds of these modules are beyond the standard default motherboard and chipset speeds, you won't see any advantage to using these unless you are overclocking your system to match.

Table 3   Overclocked (Non-JEDEC) DDR2 Module (240-Pin DIMM) Speeds and Transfer Rates

Module Standard	Chip Type	Clock Speed (MHz)	Cycles per Clock	Bus Speed (MTps)	Bus Width (Bytes)	Transfer Rate (MBps)	Dual-Channel Transfer Rate (MBps)
PC2-6000	DDR2-750	375	2	750	8	6000	12,000
PC2-7200	DDR2-900	450	2	900	8	7200	14,400
PC2-8000	DDR2-1000	500	2	1000	8	8000	16,000
PC2-8800	DDR2-1100	550	2	1100	8	8800	17,600
PC2-8888	DDR2-1111	556	2	1111	8	8888	17,777
PC2-9136	DDR2-1142	571	2	1142	8	9136	18,272
PC2-9200	DDR2-1150	575	2	1150	8	9200	18,400
PC2-9600	DDR2-1200	600	2	1200	8	9600	19,200
PC2-10000	DDR2-1250	625	2	1250	8	10000	20,000

In addition to providing greater speeds and bandwidth, DDR2 has other advantages. It uses lower voltage than conventional DDR (1.8V vs. 2.5V), so power consumption and heat generation are reduced. Because of the greater number of pins required on DDR2 chips, the chips typically use fine-pitch ball grid array (FBGA) packaging rather than the thin small outline package (TSOP) chip packaging used by most DDR and conventional SDRAM chips. FPGA chips are connected to the substrate (meaning the memory module in most cases) via tightly spaced solder balls on the base of the chip.

DDR2 DIMMs resemble conventional DDR DIMMs but have more pins and slightly different notches to prevent confusion or improper installation. For example, the different physical notches prevent you from plugging a DDR2 module into a conventional DDR (or SDR) socket. DDR2 memory module designs incorporate 240 pins, significantly more than conventional DDR or standard SDRAM DIMMs.

JEDEC began working on the DDR2 specification in April 1998, and published the standard in September 2003. DDR2 chip and module production actually began in mid-2003 (mainly samples and prototypes), and the first chipsets, motherboards, and systems supporting DDR2 appeared for Intel processor–based systems in mid-2004. At that time, variations of DDR2 such as G-DDR2 (Graphics DDR2) began appearing in graphics cards, too. Mainstream motherboard chipset support for DDR2 on Intel processor–based systems appeared in 2005. Noticeable for its lack of DDR2 support through 2005 was AMD, whose Athlon 64 and Opteron processor families included integrated DDR memory controllers. AMD processor–based systems first supported DDR2 in mid-2006, with the release of socket AM2 motherboards and processors to match.

It is interesting to note that AMD was almost two years behind Intel in the transition from DDR to DDR2. This is because AMD included the memory controller in its Athlon 64 and newer processors, instead of incorporating the memory controller in the chipset north bridge as with more traditional Intel designs. Although there are advantages to integrating the memory controller in the CPU, a major disadvantage is the inability to quickly adopt new memory architectures, because doing so requires that both the processor and processor socket be redesigned. With the memory controller in the chipset, Intel can more quickly adopt newer and faster memory architectures without having to redesign existing processors. These transitional differences will likely become apparent again in the expected transition from DDR2 to DDR3 in 2008.

DDR3 SDRAM

DDR3 is the latest JEDEC memory standard, which will enable higher levels of performance along with lower power consumption and higher reliability than DDR2. JEDEC began working on the DDR3 specification in June 2002, and the first DDR3 memory modules and supporting chipsets (Intel 3xx series) were released for Intel-based systems in late 2007. AMD is expected to introduce new processors and sockets supporting DDR3 memory sometime during 2008. Initially, DDR3 will be more expensive than DDR2, and will be used in systems requiring extremely high-performance memory. DDR3 is expected to achieve mainstream status in the 2008 to 2009 time frame.

DDR3 modules use advanced signal designs including self-driver calibration and data synchronization, along with an optional on-board thermal sensor. DDR3 memory runs on only 1.5V, which is nearly 20% less than the 1.8V used by DDR2 memory. The lower voltage combined with higher efficiency is expected to reduce overall power consumption by up to 30% compared to DDR2.

DDR3 modules are expected to initially become popular for systems where the processor/memory bus runs at 1333MHz, which is faster than the 1066MHz maximum supported by DDR2. For higher-speed memory in standard (nonoverclocked) systems, DDR3 modules rated PC3-10600 and PC3-12800 will allow for throughputs of 10,667MBps and 12,800MBps respectively. When combined in dual-channel operation, a pair of PC3-12800 modules will result in a total throughput of an incredible 25,600MBps. Table 4 shows the various official JEDEC-approved DDR2 module types and bandwidth specifications.

Table 4   JEDEC Standard DDR3 Module (240-Pin DIMM) Speeds and Transfer Rates

Module Standard	Chip Type	Clock Speed (MHz)	Cycles per Clock	Bus Speed (MTps)	Bus Width (Bytes)	Transfer Rate (MBps)	Dual-Channel Transfer Rate (MBps)
PC3-6400	DDR3-800	400	2	800	8	6400	12,800
PC3-8500	DDR3-1066	533	2	1066	8	8533	17,066
PC3-10600	DDR3-1333	667	2	1333	8	10,667	21,333
PC3-12800	DDR3-1600	800	2	1600	8	12,800	25,600

The 240-pin DDR3 modules are similar in the pin count, size, and shape to the DDR2 modules, but DDR3 modules are incompatible with DDR2 circuits, and are designed with different keying to make them physically noninterchangeable.

Dual Inline Memory Modules

Figures 4 and 5 show a 240-pin DDR2 dual inline memory module (DIMM) and 240-pin DDR3 DIMM, respectively. The pins are numbered from left to right and are different on each side. Note that all dimensions are in both inches and millimeters (in parentheses).

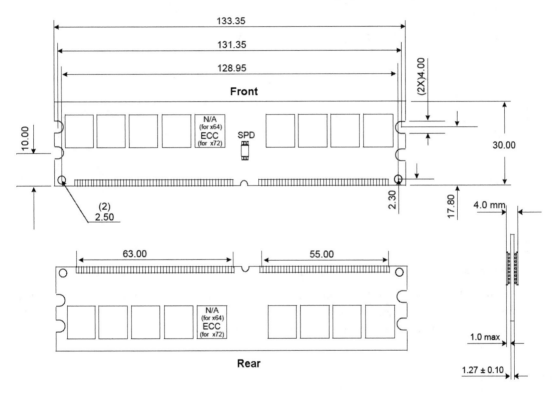

Figure 4 240-pin DDR2 DIMM dimensions.

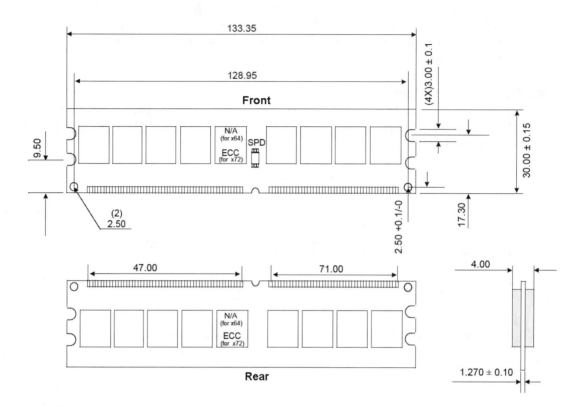

Figure 5   240-pin DDR3 DIMM dimensions.

Note that the DDR2 and DDR3 DIMMs are virtually identical in size, but they are completely different electrically and are not interchangeable. The notch or key near the center of the DIMMs is in a different position to prevent DDR2 DIMMs from being installed in DDR3 sockets and vice versa.

Memory Recommendations

For most normal installations, memory speeds are automatically read from the SPD (Serial Presence Detect) chip on the modules, which allows the motherboard to properly establish the correct settings. Many motherboards allow you to override these settings, which enables over-clocking of the memory.

In general, I recommend using the default settings (auto mode), and for the most cost-effective setup, purchase DDR2 modules in matched pairs, which allows dual-channel operation. In most cases, installing memory faster than PC2-5300 (667MHz) or PC2-6400 (800MHz) will add a great deal to the cost, while only adding a small amount of additional performance.

If you are using a 32-bit OS such as 32-bit versions of Windows XP or Vista, I recommend installing from 1 to 3GB total. The 32-bit editions of Windows XP and Vista support 4GB of physical memory. What many don't realize is that PC system hardware uses some or all of the fourth gigabyte for things such as the BIOS, motherboard resources, memory-mapped I/O, PCI configuration space, device memory (graphics aperture), VGA memory, and so on. This means that if you install 4GB (or more) RAM, most or all of the fourth gigabyte would be disabled because it is already occupied. This is called the 3GB limit and is exactly analogous to the 640K memory limit we had in the 1980s. Back then, the system supported 1M, but the upper 384K was already in use by the system.

Can any of that memory be reclaimed? For those running a 32-bit OS, the answer is definitely no. However, when running a 64-bit OS on systems that support remapping, the answer is yes. Most newer motherboard chipsets have a feature that can remap the otherwise-disabled RAM from the fourth gigabyte to the fifth (or higher) gigabyte, where it will be both visible and usable by a 64-bit OS. Note however that if the motherboard doesn't support remapping, even when running a 64-bit OS the memory will be lost.

Unfortunately, limited 64-bit driver availability as well as the inability to run legacy 16-bit code means that 64-bit OS is still not recommended for general use.

Note that the 3GB limit is not as strictly defined as it was with the 640K limit. This means that if you do install 4GB, you might get to use as much as 3.5GB of it, or possibly as little as 2.85GB or less. It depends largely on the types of buses in the system and the type and number of video cards installed. With a single low-end video card, you may have access to 3.5GB, but on a newer system with dual PCIe x16 slots, and especially with two high-end PCI Express video cards installed, you may drop the usable limit to 2.85GB or less. That means that even if you only install 3GB, you might not be able to use all of it.

Tip

Bottom line: If you are running 32-bit editions of Windows XP or Vista, I recommend installing a maximum of 3GB RAM, because most if not all of the fourth gigabyte will be unusable.

Hard Disk Drives

Most modern motherboards support up to 4, 6 or 8 Serial ATA (SATA) interface drives. Most also have support for up to two Parallel ATA (PATA) drives. A typical installation will be one or two hard disk drives (HDDs), along with a single optical disk drive (ODD). Because until recently there haven't been many SATA optical drives on the market, common practice has been to install the HDDs on the SATA interface, with optical drives on the PATA interface. However, with the advent of more SATA optical drives, today it is possible to install a system using all SATA drives.

Selecting hard drives has become a little bit more complicated in recent years. For example, I've seen compatibility problems between certain drives and chipsets due to speed negotiation problems with second generation (3.0Gbps) drives and first-generation (1.5Gbps) chipsets. In those cases, the solution was to lock the drive at 1.5Gbps via the use of a jumper or manufacturer-specific software, such as the Drive Feature Tool (DFT) program for Hitachi drives. Current chipsets (and motherboards) support the 3.0Gbps speed, so that should not be a problem with new system builds, but there can be other problems, especially related to RAID installations.

When installing one or two SATA HDDs in a normal non-RAID configuration, almost any drive will suffice; if using RAID, however, I have found that it pays to purchase only drives rated for this type of duty, which are normally categorized as "enterprise class" or "RAID edition" drives. This has to do with problems in three major areas:

- Error handling
- Acoustic and power management
- Spread-spectrum clocking

These problems are explained in the following sections.

Error Handling

Many people may be surprised to hear this, but minor read/write errors occur on hard drives all the time, which are normally corrected by the ECC (error correction code) and other recovery routines built in to the drive. Because they are automatically corrected, you don't normally see or hear anything about them during normal drive operation. In some cases, however, these errors can take up to a minute or two to correct, during which you might notice a temporary hesitation or slowdown in the system. Unfortunately, if this occurs when the drive is installed in a RAID array, the drive will likely be dropped from the array, causing the array to become degraded or fail entirely. So-called enterprise class or RAID edition drives have special TLER (time-limited error recovery) routines, which limit the amount of time the drive will spend recovering from an error to only a few seconds, thus preventing the drive from being dropped from the array.

Acoustic and Power Management

Many drives implement aggressive acoustic/power management, which intentionally slows down a drive during seeking and during periods of inactivity. Although beneficial for single-drive installations to keep drives cooler and quieter, this can cause timeouts or disruptions when drives are mounted in RAID arrays. Enterprise class or RAID edition drives are designed to either disable or minimize these effects, thus preventing array problems. Most drive manufacturers provide manufacturer-specific utilities to control or disable these functions. Note that disabling acoustic/power management may increase the thermal output of a drive, so it is important to ensure that your chassis or enclosure provides proper cooling.

Spread-Spectrum Clocking

As the clock circuits in computers and related devices have increased in speed, so has the level of EMI (electromagnetic interference) that they radiate. As a method of reducing EMI, many drives implement spread-spectrum clocking (SSC), which is a technique that slightly varies the clock frequency up and down a few percent, so as to literally spread out the EMI peak by varying the frequency. Although it does help to minimize EMI, this fluctuating clock speed can cause problems with interface circuits that aren't designed to handle it, and can cause a loss of synchronization that lowers performance and may even result in a drive being dropped from an array. Enterprise class or RAID edition drives normally have SSC disabled, and even when using standard drives without an array, I recommend disabling SSC for maximum performance. SSC can be disabled by either setting a jumper or using a manufacturer-specific utility program.

Hard Drive Reliability

Many people may be surprised to find out that most standard hard drives are not designed for 24/7 operation! On the other hand, that is exactly what enterprise class or RAID edition drives are designed for. In addition, the enterprise class or RAID edition drives are normally designed to a higher standard of reliability than conventional drives, as exhibited by significantly longer MTBF (mean time before failure) ratings, which are usually near double that of their standard counterparts. Enterprise/RAID drives are also normally rated for 10 times fewer uncorrectable errors for the same bits read. Finally, they are designed to withstand much higher tolerances of vibration, because running multiple drives in close proximity can allow the vibrations from one drive to cause read/write errors in the others.

Hard Drive Recommendations

If you have no intention of ever using drives in an array, standard drives are fine; if you will be running two or more drives in a RAID array, however, I would insist on enterprise class or RAID edition drives for maximum reliability. The enterprise class drives cost up to 25% more than their standard counterparts, but they are definitely worth it if you are using them in an array.

The following manufacturers offer both standard and enterprise class drives that I recommend for new system builds:

> Hitachi: http://www.hitachigst.com
>
> Samsung: http://www.samsung.com/global/business/hdd
>
> Seagate: http://www.seagate.com
>
> Western Digital: http://www.wdc.com

In general, I recommend using drives of 250GB to 750GB in capacity for the greatest value. There are smaller and larger drives, but you generally pay more per gigabyte outside of that range. Most SATA interface drives in this capacity range will have the following specifications:

- 7200rpm
- 4.16ms average latency
- 3Gbps external transfer rate (second-generation SATA)
- 16MB buffer (cache)
- Native Command Queuing (NCQ)
- Fluid Dynamic Bearings (FDB)
- Perpendicular Magnetic Recording (PMR)

Normally I would recommend purchasing two drives at a minimum, with one internal and one in an external enclosure for backup purposes. For additional performance, reliability, or both, you can install two or more drives internally and configure them in a RAID array. Using the Matrix RAID functionality in the Intel chipsets, you can even create different RAID volumes on the same array.

Finally, note that some SATA hard drives have both standard peripheral power connectors and SATA power connectors. If this is the case, you must plug in only one or the other. If the drives you choose have only SATA power connectors, you must ensure that your power supply has sufficient SATA power connectors, or you may need SATA power adapters.

Optical Disk Drives (DVD and CD)

In general, you will want at least one optical drive in the system, preferably a DVD+/-RW DL (dual-layer) burner. This will enable you to read and write CDs and both single- and dual-layer DVDs of all types. These drives are available in both PATA and SATA versions.

Some issues to consider with optical drives include the following:

- Bootable CD motherboard Flash BIOS upgrades might not work with SATA optical drives.

- SATA optical drives might have only SATA power connectors instead. Check your power supply to see that you have sufficient SATA power connectors. If you don't, you might need to purchase SATA power adapter cables (some drives include an adapter).

- Some drives include useful commercial CD/DVD burning and packet-writing software such as Nero and InCD, which usually works much better than the standard disc-writing capabilities built in to Windows.

- If you do a lot of disc-to-disc copying or duplicating, you might want to install two optical drives.

- Not all models provide LightScribe or DVD-RAM support; so if you need those features, be sure to check for them.

In most cases, you can get top-quality, high-speed optical-burning drives in the $30 price range.

Video Segment 3: What to Look for in a Chassis

One of the most difficult-to-select components is the chassis (commonly referred to as the case). Because so many different attributes go into the design of the chassis, no single one can possibly serve all purposes. That said, most uses can be satisfied by mini-tower or mid-tower designs. However, even among a single category such as a mini-tower, the variations are virtually infinite, and I have yet to find a single unit that has everything I want.

The best you can do is to understand all the different features and options, decide which of these features/options are the most important, and select your chassis based on those features/options. Mini-tower chassis are defined as those supporting microATX form factor motherboards. Most mid-tower chassis, on the other hand, support both microATX and full-size ATX motherboards.

In general, I prefer to build mini-tower systems because they hold more than enough of the components I need to use, and yet can be expanded to support items such as dual optical drives, as many as four to six hard disk drives, four adapter cards, and more. With that in mind, here are some of the functions and features I look for in a chassis:

- ATX or microATX motherboard form factor
- Removable motherboard tray
- High quality 300W+ ATX 2.x PSU
- 120mm or 92mm rear fan
- Provisions for front fan (HDD cooling)
- Tool-free design
- Front-panel reset switch (optional)
- Chassis air guide (CAG) = CPU side vent
- 2 to 4+ internal HDD bays
- 2+ external ODD bays
- 1+ external floppy bay
- Rounded interior edges
- Easily removable front panel
- Removable back side panel
- High-quality fit and finish

I have a love/hate relationship with front-panel ports. My dream case would have only two front USB ports, and *no* audio or FireWire ports. This is because many of the motherboards I use don't have these ports built in, and I can't stand having ports on the front of a system that are non-functional. My dream case would also have two external 3.5" floppy drive bays, not for floppy drives, but for things such as configurable front-panel port adapters, card readers, fan controllers, and more. Unfortunately, these days it seems that all the cases on the market have front-panel audio, and it often isn't compatible with my motherboard, which means in many cases that the microphone jack won't work at all, and the headphone jack won't shut off the rear speaker output when the headphones are plugged in. So, with respect to ports, I'd like the following:

- 2 USB front-panel ports.
- No integrated audio or FireWire front-panel ports. (I'd rather add these myself as necessary.)
- If audio ports are included, they should support the HD Audio standard.
- Front-panel eSATA (optional).

Although I have yet to find a case that has everything just the way I like, here are two I can recommend.

ENERMAX Chassis

One of my current favorites, these Enermax chassis are excellent overall, and are one of the few I've seen with properly designed front-panel connectors including HD Audio (headphone/mic) ports. They meet most of my criteria, with a few exceptions. The biggest exceptions being that are that they aren't completely tool-less designs, and they don't have a removable motherboard tray.

Visit the following sites to look at the specs:

> ECA2020 Vostok microATX ($66)
>
> http://www.enermax.com.tw/english/product_cases_detail.asp?PrID=79
>
> http://www.newegg.com/Product/Product.aspx?Item=N82E16811124127
>
> ECA3120 Vostok full ATX ($70)
>
> http://www.enermax.com.tw/english/product_cases_detail.asp?PrID=78
>
> http://www.newegg.com/Product/Product.aspx?Item=N82E16811124126

Foxconn Chassis

I've liked these Foxconn chassis for several years now. They meet most of my criteria, albeit with a few exceptions. The biggest exception being that the front-panel audio connections are AC-97 and not HD Audio. This unfortunately means that the microphone and headphone jacks won't work properly with most 2005 and newer motherboards. Later in this booklet, I discuss some ways of dealing with that.

> TV-544 microATX ($66)
>
> http://www.foxconnchannel.com/product/Chassis/detail_overview.aspx?ID=en-us0000049
>
> http://www.newegg.com/Product/Product.aspx?Item=N82E16811153072
>
> TP-544 full ATX ($135)
>
> http://www.foxconnchannel.com/product/Chassis/detail_overview.aspx?ID=en-us0000046
>
> http://www.newegg.com/Product/Product.aspx?Item=N82E16811153084

Superior Cooling

The fans that come in most chassis are standard sleeve-bearing models, which in some cases can be louder than I like. When building systems, I often choose to replace the fans that come with a given chassis with higher-quality fans that use fluid bearings for quieter operation and longer life.

Most motherboards have three fan connectors: one for the processor, one for a rear fan, and one for a front fan. Some motherboards may add a fourth connector for an additional fan. If you want more fans than there are motherboard fan connectors, you can purchase fans that plug into standard peripheral (that is, disk drive) power connectors. The only drawback to these is that they cannot be monitored by the motherboard fan sensors, which sense the fan speeds of fans plugged into the motherboard fan connectors only.

Most motherboard fan connectors are 3-pin types, which feature a +12V, ground, and tachometer signal. The +12V and ground are used to run the motor, and the tachometer signal is used to monitor the fan speed. Some motherboards feature 4-wire fan connectors, either for the CPU fan only, or possibly for the others, too. The 4-wire connectors add a PWM (pulse width modulation) signal, which is used to control the fan speed of 4-wire fans. Note that you can plug a 4-wire fan into a 3-wire connector, in which case the PWM signal will not be used. You can also plug a 3-wire fan into a 4-wire connector and again it will work fine without the PWM signal.

Rear Fan

I like the rear fan in a chassis to be 120mm if possible, because larger fans flow more air while running quieter and at slower speeds. If a 120mm fan is not an option, than a 92mm fan is the next best choice.

Front Fan

I like the front fan to be smaller than the rear because the front fan is designed to blow into the case, whereas the rear is designed to exhaust (blow out) of the case. You always want more air being drawn out of the case than being blown in, which keeps a negative pressure on the inside of the case that promotes proper ventilation throughout.

The front fan is primarily designed for cooling the HDDs, and I like to purchase cases where the placement of the fan will draw air in and blow directly across the drives. If you are only installing a single hard drive, or maybe just two drives, you might not need a front fan. If you are installing three or more drives in close proximity to each other, however, adding a front fan to cool them is highly recommended.

Chassis Air Guide or Processor Duct

One cost-effective way to improve heatsink performance is to reduce the ambient temperature around the processor, which means lowering the temperature of air entering the heatsink. To ensure proper cooling for their boxed (retail) processors, Intel and AMD specify maximum temperature limits for the air that enters the heatsink fan assembly. If the air temperature entering the heatsink goes over that amount, the heatsink will not be able to adequately cool the processor. Because they must account for extreme circumstances, all modern systems and heatsinks are designed to operate properly if the external environmental ambient temperature in the room is 35°C (95°F). This means that, in general, PCs are designed to work in environments of up to that temperature. To operate in environments with higher temperatures than that, more specialized designs are required. Table 5 shows the maximum heatsink air inlet temperatures allowed for various processors with factory-installed heatsinks.

Table 5   Maximum Heatsink Inlet Temperatures for Various Processors

Environmental Temperature	Maximum Heatsink Inlet Temperature	Processor Type
35°C (95°F)	45°C (113°F)	AMD K6, Pentium I, II, III
35°C (95°F)	42°C (107.6°F)	AMD Athlon, XP, 64, 64 FX
35°C (95°F)	40°C (104°F)	Pentium 4 Willamette, Northwood
35°C (95°F)	38°C (100.4°F)	Pentium 4 Northwood 3GHz+, Prescott 2.4GHz+

As you can see, for a long time new processors continually made more demands on system cooling. With the recent trend on the part of Intel and AMD to increase speed through chip design rather than pure clock speed increases, this trend has reach a plateau in a manner of speaking. The most demanding processors today require that the internal chassis temperature remain at or below 38°C (100.4°F), even if the system is running in a room temperature of 35°C (95°F). The internal temperature rise, or preheating of air inside the system, is typically caused by heat from components such as motherboard chipsets, graphics cards, memory, voltage regulators, disk drives, and other heat-generating components (including the processor itself). Even with all these devices producing heat, the specifications for many newer processors require that the air temperature inside the chassis at the heatsink can rise only to 3°C (5.4°F) over ambient. This places extreme demands on the chassis cooling.

Chassis that have been specifically designed to improve cooling for the processor by maintaining a temperature of 38°C or less at the processor heatsink inlet are often referred to as thermally advantaged chassis (TAC). Using a TAC both allows the processor to remain cool even under extreme environmental conditions and helps reduce noise. Most modern processors and chassis incorporate cooling systems that can adjust the speeds of the fans. If the temperatures remain below specific limits, the fans run at lower speeds, thus reducing the noise level. If temperatures rise, so do fan speeds and noise. In general, TACs enable fan speeds to remain lower, resulting in quieter operation.

One of the simplest ways to enable a chassis to meet the TAC guidelines is to add a duct or air guide directly over the processor. This is called a *processor duct* or *chassis air guide*, and it essentially enables the processor heatsink to draw air directly from outside the chassis, greatly improving the thermal performance of the processor heatsink and easily meeting the requirement for a 38°C or lower heatsink inlet temperature. The specifications for this duct, and for an additional vent in the side cover for adapter cards such as graphics boards, can be found in an official standard called the Chassis Air Guide (CAG) Design Guide, which was initially published in May 2002 and revised in September 2003. This guide details the dimensions and locations of the processor duct (and other attributes of the design). Figure 6 shows a typical tower chassis with the processor duct installed in the side cover.

The processor duct is essentially a tube positioned directly over the processor heatsink, allowing it to pull cool air from outside the chassis. When viewed from the side, the duct is usually covered by a grill or vent cover. Figure 7 shows the processor duct and adapter card vents as viewed from the side.

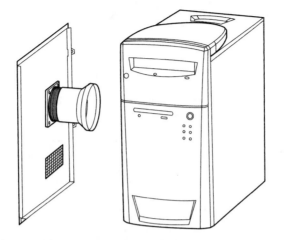

Figure 6   TAC featuring a processor air duct and adapter card vent in the side cover.

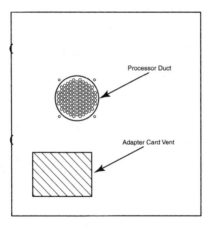

Processor Duct

Adapter Card Vent

Figure 7   TAC processor duct and adapter card vent as viewed from the side.

The processor duct is the most important part of the TAC design, and the placement of the duct is critical to its performance. The duct must be centered over the processor heatsink, and it must be positioned such that the end of the duct is spaced 12mm to 20mm from the top of the heatsink. This ensures that the processor heatsink ingests only cool air from outside the chassis and enables some air to spill over to cool other parts of the system. Figure 8 shows the duct placement in relation to the top of the processor heatsink.

Because chassis can vary in size, shape, and dimension, the CAG standard details the placement of the processor duct and adapter card vent in relation to an industry-standard ATX motherboard.

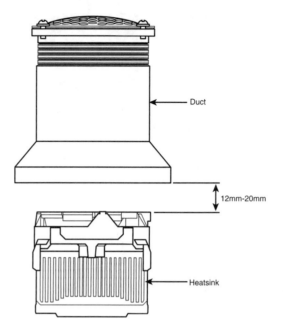

Figure 8 Processor air duct placement in relation to the processor heatsink.

The effect of the processor duct is quite noticeable in system operation. In a study done by Intel, it tested a system running Windows XP with a 3GHz Pentium 4 processor, a D865PERL mother-board, a GeForce4 video card, DDR400 memory, a hard drive, a CD-ROM drive, a sound card, and both rear- and front-mounted 80mm fans. The system was running in a 25°C (77°F) room, and the test results were as follows:

	Without CPU Duct	**With CPU Duct**
CPU inlet temp.	35°C (95°F)	28°C (82.4°F)
CPU fan speed	4050rpm	2810rpm
Sound level	39.8dBA	29.9dBA

As you can see, adding the duct dropped the temperature of the processor by 7°C (12.6°F), even while allowing the heatsink fan speed to drop to the lowest setting. The result is a processor that runs cooler, a fan that lasts longer, and less noise. As you can see, even with dual-chassis fans already in the system, the processor duct makes a huge difference.

Note that it is possible to have a TAC without the processor air duct, as long as the chassis meets the TAC temperature guidelines. By selecting a thermally advantaged chassis, you ensure that your processor remains cool under the most extreme environmental conditions, not to mention that you extend the life of the heatsink fan and cause your system to be much quieter overall.

Power Supply

I have always placed great emphasis on selecting a power supply for my systems. I consider the power supply the core of the system and am willing to spend more to get a more robust and reliable unit. The power supply is critical because it supplies electrical power to every other component in the system. In my experience, the power supply is also one of the most failure-prone components in any computer system. I have replaced more power supplies in PCs than any other part. This is especially because, to keep system prices down, many system builders use the cheapest power supplies they can find. A malfunctioning power supply can cause other components in the system to malfunction, and it can also damage the other components in your computer by delivering improper or erratic voltages. Because of its importance to proper and reliable system operation, you should understand both the function and limitations of a power supply, and its potential problems and their solutions.

Most PCs today use power supplies that conform to the ATX12V or EPS form factor standards. These standards dictate the shape of the power supply and the types of connectors they should have. Figure 9 shows the ATX12V 2.x form factor, which is currently the most popular.

Other variations on this design are possible. For example, although the width and height are standard, the depth can vary according to these standards:

- 101mm deep = PS3 (short ATX12V)
- 140mm deep = standard ATX12V
- 180mm or 230mm deep = EPS (entry-level server power supply)

The types of main power connectors between the power supply and the motherboard can vary according to the standard, too:

- 20-pin main and 4-pin +12V (ATX12V 1.x)
- 24-pin main and 4-pin +12V (ATX12V 2.x)
- 24-pin main and 8-pin +12V (EPS)

Standard power supplies will normally have at least four additional types of connectors, too:

- PCIe video power
- SATA power
- Peripheral power
- Floppy power

You can see the 24-pin main and 4-pin +12V (ATX12V 2.x) in Figure 9, which depicts a typical ATX12V 2.x standard supply.

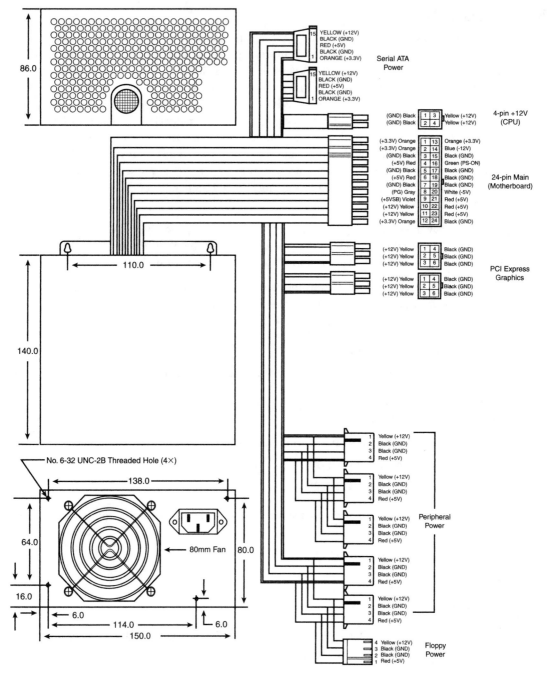

Figure 9 ATX12V 2.x form factor power supply with 24-pin main, 4-pin +12V, and optional PCI Express Graphics connectors.

Unfortunately, many of the power supplies included with less-expensive cases are low-quality units. If your chassis didn't come with a power supply, or you want to upgrade the basic unit that was included to something with more power output and reliability, I highly recommend power supplies from PC Power and Cooling: http://pcpower.com.

Here are some of the units I recommend:

- Silencer 470 ($80)
  - 140mm deep
  - One 6-pin PCIe video power
  - 74% efficient
  - 9 drive connectors (3 SATA, 5 Molex, 1 mini)
- Silencer 610 ($120)
  - 180mm deep
  - One 8-pin CPU power
  - Two 6-pin PCIe video power
  - 83% efficient
  - 15 drive connectors (6 SATA, 8 Molex, 1 mini)
- Silencer 750 ($200)
  - 180mm deep
  - One 8-pin CPU power
  - Two 6-pin PCIe video power
  - Two 6/8-pin PCIe video power
  - 83% efficient
  - 15 drive connectors (6 SATA, 8 Molex, 1 mini)
- Turbo-Cool 1KW-SR ($460)
  - 230mm deep
  - Two 8-pin CPU power
  - Two 6-pin PCIe video power
  - Two 6/8-pin PCIe video power
  - 83% efficient
  - 15 drive connectors (6 SATA, 8 Molex, 1 mini)

Most systems can easily get by with the 470W unit, but for builds using high-powered video cards, or especially those with dual video cards, you might want to consider one of the higher-output units.

Chassis Front-Panel Connections

In general, four main types of front-panel connectors are found on modern motherboards:

- Switch/LED
- USB
- Audio
- FireWire

These are all supposed to be implemented via keyed 10-pin header connectors on the mother-board, and matching 10-pin plugs on the chassis.

Switch/LED Connector

The switch/LED connector is used to connect the power and reset buttons and the power and HDD LEDs on the chassis front panel to the motherboard. The pinout and configuration of the

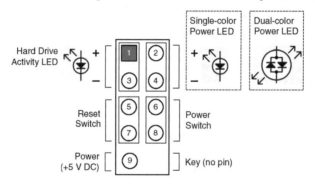

switch/LED connector is shown in Figure 10 and Table 6.

Figure 10   Switch/LED front-panel header connector configuration.

Table 6   Switch/LED Front-Panel Header Connector Pinout

Pin	Signal	Description	Wire Color
1	HD_PWR	Hard disk LED +5V	Orange
2	HDR_BLNK_GRN	Power LED +5V/Standby	Green
3	HDA#	Hard disk active	White
4	HDR_BLNK_YEL	Power on/Standby LED +5V	White
5	Ground	Ground (reset switch)	White
6	FPBUT_IN#	Power switch	Red
7	FP_RESET#	Reset switch	Purple
8	Ground	Ground (power switch)	White
9	+5V	Power (not connected)	N/A
10	Key (no pin)	N/A	N/A

Some chassis will include individual 2-pin power connectors for the switches and LED. In that case, you must be careful to connect each one properly. In particular, when making the LED connections, you must observe proper polarity. Note that few manufacturers seem to follow the wire color codes. In general, however, the LED connections will use a white wire for negative, and the colored wire will be positive. If you reverse them, no damage will occur, but the LED won't work properly. Switch connections essentially have no polarity, and the orientation of the white/colored wires doesn't really matter.

USB Connectors

Most motherboards include multiple on-board USB header connectors, which are designed to be connected to front-mounted or rear-bracket USB connectors in the chassis. The standard uses a single 10-pin keyed connector to provide *2* USB connections, with each port connection using only 4 pins in the connector. The pinout and configuration of a standard dual-USB motherboard header connector is shown in Figure 11 and Table 7.

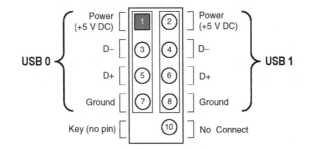

Figure 11   Dual-USB header connector configuration.

Table 7   Dual-USB Header Connector Pinout

Pin	Signal Names	Description	Wire Color
1	USB0_PWR	Port 0 +5V power	Red
2	USB1_PWR	Port 1 +5V power	Red
3	USB_D0-	Port 0 Data-	White
4	USB_D1-	Port 1 Data-	White
5	USB_D0+	Port 0 Data+	Green
6	USB_D1+	Port 1 Data+	Green
7	GND	Port 0 Ground	Black
8	GND	Port 1 Ground	Black
9	Key (no pin)	N/A	N/A
10	NC/Shield	No Connect/Shield	N/A / Blue

Note that many manufacturers don't follow these color codes exactly; they are here only for general guidelines. Many chassis include multiple inline connectors for the dual USB–to–front panel or rear bracket connections rather than a single-keyed connector. They might use individually labeled pins, or two 4-pin inline connectors, with one for each port. In some cases, there will be extra ground wires, too, which can be left disconnected.

Caution

If your chassis uses multiple individual nonkeyed connections, you must be sure to connect them properly to the connector on the motherboard. If you connect them improperly (especially backward), you can cause a short circuit to occur that can damage the motherboard or any USB peripherals you plug into the front-panel connectors. Higher-quality motherboards usually have self-healing fuses on the power signals, which can prevent damage if such a situation occurs.

Audio Connectors

Motherboards that have integrated audio hardware usually feature a front-panel audio header connector, which is usually color coded yellow. There are two standards for this connector, depending on the type of audio built in to the motherboard, which is dependent on the motherboard chipset and relative age of the motherboard.

Motherboards using Intel 9xx series and newer (including 3x series) chipsets incorporate a standard called HD (High Definition) Audio (codenamed Azalia), whereas motherboards using Intel 8xx series and earlier chipsets usually incorporated a standard called AC'97 (Audio Codec 1997). This means that older motherboards with integrated audio built from 1997 through 2004 usually include AC'97 Audio, whereas motherboards with integrated audio from 2005 to the present usually include HD Audio.

HD Audio Connectors

The front-panel connector pinout and configuration for HD Audio is shown in Figure 12 and Table 8.

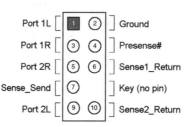

Figure 12   HD Audio front-panel audio header connector configuration.

Table 8   HD Audio Front-Panel Header Connector Pinout

Pin	Signal Name	Description	Wire Color
1	PORT 1L	Analog port 1 (microphone) input - left channel	Red
2	GND	Ground	Blue
3	PORT 1R	Analog port 1 (microphone) input - right channel	Orange/white
4	PRESENCE#	Signals HD Audio front ports connected (active low)	Black
5	PORT 2R	Analog port 2 (headphone) output - right channel	Brown/white
6	SENSE1_RETURN	Front-panel jack 1 (mic) detection return	Brown
7	SENSE_SEND	Front-panel jack detection sense line	Blue/white
8	KEY (no pin)	N/A	N/A
9	PORT 2L	Analog port 2 (headphone) output - left channel	White/black
10	SENSE2_RETURN	Front-panel jack 2 (headphone) detection return	Black

HD Audio includes intelligent jack detection, which allows the motherboard and audio control software to automatically detect whether you have plugged anything into the front- or rear-panel ports, and reassign the ports appropriately. If your chassis includes HD Audio front-panel jacks, you should be able to easily connect the plug for the front-panel jacks to the motherboard.

Note

Note that when searching for cases or case accessories that include audio ports, they will often describe HD Audio by its former "Azalia" codename.

AC'97 Audio Connectors

Older motherboards normally include AC'97 Audio, which is less capable, and less intelligent than HD Audio. The front-panel connector pinout and configuration for AC'97 is shown in Figure 13 and Table 9.

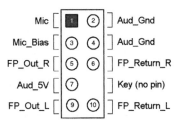

Figure 13   AC'97 Audio front-panel audio header connector configuration.

Table 9   AC'97 Audio Front-Panel Header Connector Pinout

Pin	Signal Name	Description	Wire Color
1	MIC	Analog port 1 (microphone) input – left channel	Red
2	AUD_GND	Ground (microphone)	Black
3	MIC_BIAS	Analog port 1 (microphone) input - right channel	White
4	AUD_GND	Ground	N/A
5	FP_OUT_R	Analog port 2 (headphone) output - right channel	Orange
6	FP_RETURN_R	Right channel return (w/headphones unplugged)	Yellow
7	AUD_5V	Filtered +5 V used by analog audio circuits	N/A
8	KEY (no pin)	N/A	N/A
9	FP_OUT_L	Analog port 2 (headphone) output - left channel	Green
10	FP_RETURN_L	Left channel return (w/headphones unplugged)	Blue

Note that the wire color coding is not standardized throughout the industry; this is only an example of the most popular configuration. Unfortunately, in addition with AC'97, even the labeling used in both the motherboard manuals and the front-panel chassis connectors has been somewhat inconsistent, even though the actual function of the pins is a standard. Table 10 lists some of the different designations I've seen being used to describe the same AC'97 connector pins.

Table 10   AC'97 Audio Front-Panel Header Connector Pinout Showing Alternative Signal Names

Pin	Standard	Signal Name	Alternate	Signal Name
1	MIC	MIC IN	AUD_MIC	Mic In
2	AUD_GND	MIC GND	AUD_GND	Ground
3	MIC_BIAS	MIC POWER	AUD_MIC_BIAS	Mic Bias
4	AUD_GND	GND	AUD_GND	Ground
5	FP_OUT_R	HPOUT R	AUD_FPOUT_R	Right_Out
6	FP_RETURN_R	HPOUT –R	AUD_RET_R	Right_Return
7	AUD_5V	POWER	AUD_POWER	Power
8	KEY (no pin)	N/A	N/A	N/A
9	FP_OUT_L	HPOUT L	AUD_FPOUT_L	Left_Out
10	FP_RETURN_L	HPOUT –L	AUD_RET_L	Left_Return

AC'97 front ports use switches in the jacks to disconnect output from the rear ports when a microphone or headphones are plugged into the front. If you install a motherboard with an AC'97 Audio front-panel header connector in a chassis that has no front audio ports, in many cases jumpers must be placed on the ports to ensure that the signals are routed to the rear ports. Figure 14 shows how the jumpers should be placed on the AC'97 front-panel audio header if no front ports are connected.

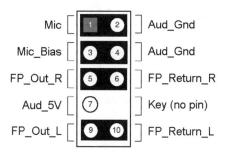

Figure 14 AC'97 Audio front-panel audio header connector jumper configuration—used when no front ports are connected.

With the jumpers installed, the front-panel audio line-out signals are routed to the back-panel audio line-out connector. With the jumpers removed, the connector provides audio line-out and mic-in signals for the front-panel audio connectors. Some motherboards with AC'97 Audio can output to the rear ports without these jumpers, but many cannot.

Whether using HD Audio or AC'97 Audio front ports, when you plug a microphone into the front-panel mic (pink) jack, it should automatically disable the rear-panel mic (pink) jack. The same goes for the front-panel headphone (green) jack; when the headphones are plugged in, the rear line-out (green) jack should be disabled.

HD Audio Motherboards and AC'97 Front Ports

The ideal situation is to have both a motherboard and chassis with HD Audio support. Unfortunately, one of the more common problems I encounter when building systems is installing a newer motherboard featuring HD Audio into an older chassis with AC'97 Audio front-panel jacks. Even many new chassis still come with AC'97 Audio front ports, even though most motherboards have been including HD Audio since 2005. Connecting an HD Audio motherboard header to an AC'97 front panel can work, but with reduced capabilities.

To make this work, connect the AC'97 front-panel ports just as you would to an AC'97 motherboard connector. Then with the HD Audio driver and audio control panel software installed (usually included on the driver disc that comes with the motherboard), go into the audio control panel and disable the front jack detection.

In my experience, with this type of setup the headphones will work, but won't disable the rear line-out (speakers) connection, meaning you'll have to mute the speakers manually when the headphones are connected. If you connect a microphone to the front mic jack, it will either work in mono mode or not work at all. If the microphone won't work when plugged into the front mic jack, you'll have to plug it into the rear for it to work.

IEEE 1394 (FireWire) Connectors

Although IEEE 1394 (FireWire/i.LINK) connectors are not found on most motherboards, some boards do incorporate this feature or offer it as an option. FireWire can also be added via an expansion card or might be included on a sound card, and many of the cards have header connectors for front-panel or rear-bracket connections similar to that found on a motherboard. Figure 15 and Table 11 show the configuration and pinout of the industry-standard FireWire header connector.

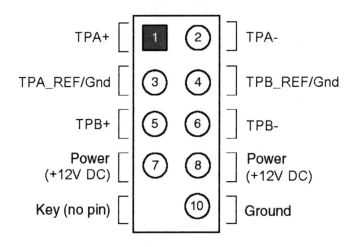

Figure 15   IEEE 1394a/b (FireWire/i.LINK) header connector configuration.

Table 11   **IEEE 1394a/b (FireWire/i.LINK) Header Connector Pinout**

Pin	Signal Name	Description	Wire Color
1	TPA+	Twisted-pair A+	Light blue
2	TPA-	Twisted-pair A-	Orange
3	GND/TPA_REF	TPA ground	Black
4	GND/TPB_REF	TPB ground	Black
5	TPB+	Twisted-pair B+	Green
6	TPB-	Twisted-pair B-	Red
7	+12V (fused)	+12V power	Blue
8	+12V (fused)	+12V power	Red
9	Key (no pin)	N/A	N/A
10	Ground	Ground	Black

Note that many manufacturers don't follow these color codes exactly; they are here only for general guidelines. Also note that motherboard and front-panel FireWire connectors are either 1394a (400MBps) or 1394b (800MBps), but not both. You should only plug a 1394b front- or rear-panel connector into a 1394b motherboard header, and likewise only connect 1394a front-panel connectors to 1394a headers. Mixing these will work in many situations, but problems can result because the external connectors are different. To facilitate proper connections, 1394a header and front/rear-panel connectors should be color coded blue, whereas 1394b header and front/rear-panel connectors should be color coded red.

Note that the FireWire header connector has the same basic physical configuration and keying as a USB connector. This is unfortunate because it enables a USB front-panel cable to be plugged into a FireWire connector, and vice versa. Either situation could cause a short circuit, resulting in possible damage to the motherboard and to any USB or FireWire peripherals.

Caution

You must not plug a USB front/rear-panel cable into a FireWire header connector, or a FireWire front/rear-panel cable into a USB header connector. Doing so causes a short circuit that can damage the motherboard and to any peripherals you plug into the front- or rear-panel connectors. Higher-quality motherboards usually have self-healing fuses on the power signals, which can prevent damage if such a situation occurs.

Connector Tips and Tricks

One of the biggest problems in system building today is dealing with front-panel connections, especially considering the variety of different motherboards and cases available. What is aggravating is that although these connectors are supposed to be defined by standards, many chassis manufacturers and some motherboard manufacturers do not follow the standards, resulting in a messy tangle of individually labeled wires and multiple tiny connectors that have to be individually connected, instead of a standard plug that makes all the connections at once. Although things are improving, many chassis manufacturers seem to be late in getting with the program, leaving us to suffer with tedious and messy connections between the front-panel chassis switches, LEDs, and ports, and the corresponding connectors on the motherboard. Fortunately, I can show you how to solve the problem by converting any individual 1-, 2-, or 4-pin front-panel connectors intended for a single 2x5 header into single 10-pin plug-in connector solution that directly attaches to the motherboard headers with a minimum of hassle.

Header Connectors

The header connectors used on motherboards are known as 2x5 (10-pin) 0.100" (2.54mm) pin header connectors. The male part of the connector is normally soldered onto the motherboard, with the open pins sticking up from the board. An example of this can be seen in Figure 16.

Figure 16   Standard 2x5 (10-pin) 0.100" (2.54mm) pin header (keyed).

Note how the pins are numbered from 1 to 10, with this particular example missing pin 10 for keying purposes. The mating connector would normally have a plug in the pin 10 position, thus preventing it from attaching backward. The key pin 10 in this example indicates that this header is for the front-panel switch/LED connection; other connectors have different keying according to Table 12.

Table 12   Motherboard 2x5 (10-pin) Header Connector Key Pins and Colors

2x5 (10-pin) header	Key Pin	Header Color
Switch/LED connector	10	Black/multi
Dual-USB connector	9	Black
Audio connector	8	Yellow
1394a FireWire connector	9	Blue
1394b FireWire connector	9	Red

Note that the USB and FireWire headers use the same key pins, which is somewhat dangerous because they are not electrically compatible. Different color coding is generally used on the motherboard headers to distinguish them, but not all chassis and motherboard manufacturers follow the codes.

To simplify front panel–to–motherboard connections, rather than attaching several smaller connectors to one of these 10-pin headers, we can replace the multiple connectors with a single 2x5 female connector that connects all the pins at once.

An example of a 2x5 connector housing is shown in Figure 17.

Figure 17   Standard 2x5 (10-pin) 0.100" (2.54mm) pin female connector housing.

These 2x5 (10-pin) connector housings are available from virtually all electronics suppliers in quantities, but they can be ordered from FrontX.com in small or even single-unit quantities under FrontX part number CPX075-4: http://frontx.com/cpx075_4.html.

You will need one of these housings for each 2x5 switch/LED, dual-USB, audio, or FireWire header connectors you want to convert. Note that the housings are generally available only in black, and because all holes will be open, the standard keying won't be in effect. You can order polarizing plugs to block the key pins on the connectors you assemble. Unfortunately, they are not available from FrontX, but you can get them from suppliers such as Digi-Key, Mouser, Newark Electronics, or other electronics parts suppliers under Molex part number 15-04-0292 for just a few cents each. After you have the connector housings (and optional polarizing plugs), you are ready to convert your connections in seconds. I've been doing this to all the chassis I use in all the systems I've been building for several years now. Let's start with the standard switch/LED connectors.

Switch/LED

Most motherboards have an industry-standard 10-pin switch/LED header connector for the front-panel switch/LED connections, but many if not most chassis continue to provide individual 2-pin connectors for the power/reset switches and power/HDD LEDs. If 2-pin connectors are used for all of these connections, they can be difficult to connect properly in the dimly lit confines of the chassis, resulting in LEDs and switches that don't work properly or at all. In addition, because a 2-pin connector can't be keyed, people often plug the LED connections in backward, which while not causing any damage, will render the LEDs inoperable. Fortunately, if you encounter such a situation, you can easily replace the multiple 2-pin connectors with a single 10-pin connector shell, making the front-panel connections a breeze. Figures 18 and 19 show the before and after results of both the connectors and the motherboard connection.

Figure 18 Separate 1x2 (2-pin) switch/LED connectors (left), replaced by a single 2x5 (10-pin) connector (right).

Figure 19   Motherboard switch/LED connection using a single 2x5 connector.

To accomplish this, merely follow these steps.

1. Remove the terminals from the 1x2 connector housings by gently lifting the latch on the connector shell with a small screwdriver or the blade of a pocketknife and then pulling the wire (with terminal attached) out of the housing. See Figures 20 and 21.

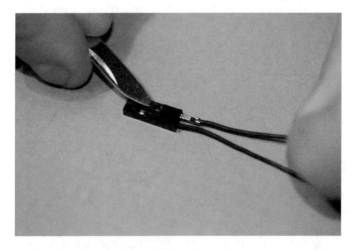

Figure 20   Use a small screwdriver or a knife blade to lift the latch.

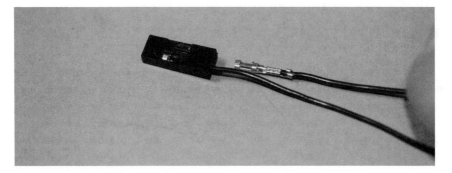

Figure 21   Gently pull the wire to remove the terminal from the header connector housing.

2. Reverse the procedure by inserting the terminals into the 2x5 connector housing according to the proper connector pinout. Make sure the terminals are fully inserted, upon which they will be locked in place by the latch on the housing. See Figures 22 and 23.

Figure 22   Inserting the terminal into a 2x5 header connector housing.

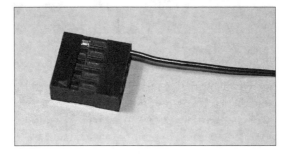

Figure 23   When the terminal is inserted, it locks into place automatically.

That's all there is to it! When you are finished, the 2x5 connector housing should have either six (if your case has no reset button) or eight terminals inserted. There should be no terminals in the pin 9 (unused) and 10 (key) positions.

The most important thing in doing this sort of operation is to keep the pinout correct in the 2x5 header. To keep things straight regarding the pinout, it is best to consult the pinout diagrams and figures in this booklet, and do each small connector one at a time. For example, take the terminals out of the 1x2 power switch connector and insert them into the 2x5 housing before moving on to the reset switch or LED connectors. If you do one small connector at a time, it will be easier to keep the pinout straight.

USB

The same thing can be accomplished with USB connectors. Many chassis come with front-panel USB connectors that either have all individual 1x1 connectors, or a pair of 1x4 connectors, sometimes accompanied by a pair of 1x1 ground wires. Just as with the switch/LED connectors, it is relatively simple to move the terminals from the 1x4 or 1x1 connectors to a single 2x5 connector. Figure 24 shows a pair of 1x1 and 1x3 connectors for a dual-USB port replaced by a single 2x5 connector.

Figure 24   Replacing dual-USB 1x1 and 1x3 connectors (left) with a single 2x5 connector (right).

To accomplish this, merely follow the same procedure as I detailed before, the only difference will be the pinout. Note that each USB port technically uses only four wires, resulting in a total of eight wires in the 2x5 connector housing. When you have finished, there should be no terminals in the pin 9 (key) or pin 10 (unused) positions. Note that if there are additional ground wires left over after you insert the eight terminals into the 2x5 connector, they can simply be cut off or tied up out of the way.

Audio

Most chassis that include HD Audio front-panel connectors will already have all the terminals in a single 2x5 connector housing. If your chassis includes an AC'97 Audio front panel, in many cases the terminals will be in individual 1x1 connectors. In that case, you can use the procedure I've outlined previously to move the terminals from the individual connectors to a single 2x5 housing. If you are looking for an easy way to arrive at a single connector AC'97 Audio plug-in, FrontX.com sells a complete internal AC'97 assembly under FrontX part number CPX503: http://frontx.com/cpx503.html.

If you are connecting a motherboard that has an HD Audio header to a chassis that has AC'97 front-panel audio jacks, connect the cable to the motherboard as if it were AC'97. Then, in the audio control software, turn off jack detection, and at least the headphone jack should work. I've had hit-or-miss luck getting the front microphone jack to work in that type of setup, in which case I've had to plug in into the rear microphone jack for it to work properly.

IEEE 1394 (FireWire)

If your chassis includes a FireWire connector in the front panel, in many cases the terminals will be in individual 1x1 connectors. In that case, you can use the procedure I've outlined previously to move the terminals from the individual connectors to a single 2x5 housing.

If you are looking for an easy way to arrive at a single-connector FireWire plug-in, FrontX.com sells a complete internal FireWire assembly under FrontX part number CPX501: http://frontx.com/cpx501.html.

Front-Panel Tricks

I've built hundreds of systems over the years, and have just about seen it all. When I build a system, I like it to be professional in both appearance and operation. Nothing screams "amateur" to me more than front-panel ports that either don't work at all, or that work improperly. Of course, it is easy to see why these things happen. For example, what if my chassis includes a port that my motherboard doesn't have built in? Or what if my chassis includes AC'97 Audio ports, and they don't work properly with the HD Audio header built in to my motherboard? Well, there are several creative ways you can fix these sorts of problems. I'll outline a couple of the problems that I've encountered, and give you some of my suggested solutions.

There are USB, audio, or FireWire ports on the chassis, but no corresponding built-in ports on the motherboard

When I build a system, I often wish I could configure the chassis with only the ports I want. Unfortunately, that isn't usually an option. In many situations, the chassis that are available (or that I have on hand) will have front-panel ports for which there is no corresponding port on the motherboard. For example, although most motherboards include internal USB ports, and many also include an audio header, not all include FireWire.

In the case of extraneous ports, you basically have two options: Add hardware to support them, or cover them up. To support them, you can purchase USB, sound, or FireWire cards that contain the same type of 2x5 headers that you would find on a motherboard. In some situations, I've even rerouted ports from the back panel to the front, using special cables and brackets available from companies such as FrontX.com. Some chassis are even coming with eSATA ports; and if your motherboard doesn't have eSATA connectors internally, you can add a card for that, too.

The other option for unused ports is to cover them up. Over the years, I've become adept at figuring out ways to cover up ports in cases, without making it obvious. I've used spare blank 5.25" or 3.5" black or beige plastic drive bay covers; cut pieces of rubber, plastic, or even metal sheet to make inserts that cover up existing ports; and I've even used properly sized stick-on badges (automotive emblems are my favorite) to cover up ports. One of my cases has a Chevy SS emblem on it just for that purpose. Intel actually sells (via its shop.intel.com site) black plastic plugs specifically designed to block off unused audio ports. Although they show these being used on back-panel ports, I've used them to cover nonfunctional front-panel audio microphone and headphone jacks, too: http://tinyurl.com/36yf8g.

My case has AC'97 jacks that don't work properly with the HD Audio built in to my motherboard

This is a real pet peeve of mine. Although many of the case manufacturers are upgrading to HD Audio front ports, many persist on including AC'97 ports, even though they have been out of fashion for years. One solution is to try to remove the existing audio jacks and try to replace them with jacks and circuitry that is HD Audio compatible. Unfortunately, you will see that this can prove to be very difficult given that most ports are directly built in to a circuit board mounted to the front of the case, and these boards are not usually interchangeable. Generally, I've found that the best solution is to block off the ports using the plugs or other techniques, as I mentioned in the previous section.

But what if you still want front-panel audio jacks that work? Fortunately, there is an easy solution to that, if your case has a blank 3.5" external (floppy) or 5.25" external (optical) drive bay. Front-panel adapters that install just like a disk drive are available from many companies, and these incorporate USB, FireWire, and audio jacks (including those that are HD Audio or "Azalia" compatible) built in. Some are also available with integrated media readers, fan speed controllers, temperature readouts, and numerous other features and functions. Retailers such as NewEgg.com sell many of these types of devices, which you can see here: http://tinyurl.com/2nygwq.

As you can see, a number of creative solutions are available to either add ports to a system or to cover up, delete, or block off ports that are otherwise dead or unusable. No matter what, I insist that all the visible ports be functional on any systems that I build.

Video Segment 4: System Assembly

Now we're actually ready to begin building the system! The assembly process is not an exact science. Depending on the number and types of components you are using, there are several different ways to go about it. In particular, the order you put things together is not etched in stone, but you can follow some general guidelines. For this build, I follow this basic order:

1. Prepare (completely disassemble) the chassis.

2. Install the motherboard in the tray.

3. Install the processor in the socket.

4. Install the heat sink on the processor.

5. Install the memory.

6. Install the motherboard in the chassis.

7. Install the drives in the chassis.

8. Connect the front-panel switches/LEDs/ports.

9. Install the power supply.

10. Finish the system.

11. Start up the system.

12. Configure BIOS setup.

After that, the system is fully operational from a hardware standpoint, and I'm ready to install the OS.

Tools and Chassis

The process of physically assembling a PC requires only a few basic tools: a 1/4" nut driver or Phillips-head screwdriver for the external screws that hold the cover in place and a 3/16" nut driver or Phillips-head screwdriver for all the other screws. Needle-nose pliers can also help in removing motherboard standoffs, jumpers, and stubborn cable connectors. Because of marketplace standardization, only a couple types and sizes of screws (with a few exceptions) are used to hold a system together. Also, the physical arrangement of the major components is similar even among different manufacturers. Figure 25 shows the components that go into a typical system, and Figure 26 shows the system with those components assembled. Note that the components shown here are for a standard PC. Your final component list might vary.

You'll find more information on tools used to work on PCs in Chapter 22, "PC Diagnostics, Testing, and Maintenance," of my bestselling book *Upgrading and Repairing PCs, 18th edition* (or newer).

For this build, I also used rubber gloves, which I wore to spread out the thermal interface material (TIM) or thermal grease on the top of the processor. I also used spare TIM because the stuff that comes preapplied to the heatsink on a new processor can only be used once.

Other tools you'll need at the end of the build are software related. You'll need an operating system install disc, and it is a good idea to have discs handy with any drivers, operating system service packs, or other important software you will want to install.

Figure 25 Components used in building a typical PC, including (L to R) the case, HDDs, ODD, RAM, CPU, and motherboard.

Figure 26 The completed system using all components shown in Figure 25.

ESD Protection

One issue you must be aware of is electrostatic discharge (ESD) protection. Another is recording the configuration of the system with regard to the physical aspects of the system (such as jumper or switch settings and cable orientations) and the logical configuration of the system (especially in terms of elements such as CMOS settings).

When you are working on the internal components of a computer, you must take the necessary precautions to prevent accidental static discharges to the components. At any time, your body can hold a large static voltage charge that can easily damage components of your system. Before I ever put my hands into an open system, I first touch a grounded portion of the chassis, such as the power-supply case. This action serves to equalize the electrical charges the device and my body might be carrying. Be sure the power supply is unplugged during all phases of the assembly process. Some will claim that you should leave the system plugged in to provide an earth ground through the power cord and outlet, but that is unnecessary. If you leave the system plugged in, you open yourself up to other problems, such as accidentally turning it on or leaving it on when installing a board or device, which can damage the motherboard or other devices.

Caution

Also note that power supplies used in many systems today deliver a +5V current to the motherboard continuously—that is, whenever they are plugged in. Bottom line: Be sure any system you are working on is completely unplugged from the wall outlet.

High-end workbenches at repair facilities have the entire bench grounded, so it's not as big of a problem; however, you need something to be a good ground source to prevent a current from building up in you.

A more sophisticated way to equalize the charges between you and any of the system components is to use an ESD protection kit. These kits consist of a wrist strap and mat, with ground wires for attachment to the system chassis. When you are going to work on a system, you place the mat next to or partially below the system unit. Next, you clip the ground wire to both the mat and the system's chassis, tying the grounds together. You then put on the wrist strap and attach that wire to a ground. Because the mat and system chassis are already wired together, you can attach the wrist-strap wire to the system chassis or to the mat. If you are using a wrist strap without a mat, clip the wrist-strap wire to the system chassis. When clipping these wires to the chassis, be sure to use an area that is free of paint so that a good ground contact can be achieved. This setup ensures that any electrical charges are carried equally by you and any of the components in the system, preventing the sudden flow of static electricity that can damage the circuits.

As you install or remove disk drives, adapter cards, and especially delicate items such as the entire motherboard, memory modules, or processors, you should place these components on the static mat. Sometimes people put the system unit on top of the mat, but the unit should be alongside the mat so that you have room to lay out all the components as you work with them. If you are going to remove the motherboard from a system, be sure you leave enough room for it on the mat.

If you do not have such a mat, place the removed circuits and devices on a clean desk or table. Always pick up a loose adapter card by the metal bracket used to secure the card to the system. This bracket is tied into the ground circuitry of the card, so by touching the bracket first, you prevent a discharge from damaging the components of the card. If the circuit board has no metal bracket (a motherboard, for example), handle the board carefully by the edges, and try not to touch any of the connectors or components. If you don't have proper ESD equipment such as a wrist strap or mat, be sure to periodically touch the chassis while working inside the system to equalize any charge you might have built up.

Caution

Some people recommend placing loose circuit boards and chips on sheets of aluminum foil. I absolutely *do not recommend* this procedure because it can actually result in an explosion! Many motherboards, adapter cards, and other circuit boards today have built-in lithium or NiCad batteries. These batteries react violently when they are shorted out, which is exactly what you would be doing by placing such a board on a piece of aluminum foil. The batteries will quickly overheat and possibly explode like a large firecracker (with dangerous shrapnel). Because you will not always be able to tell whether a board has a battery built in to it somewhere, the safest practice is to never place any board on any conductive metal surface.

Prepare Chassis

Now we're ready to prepare the chassis for the build. Basically this means taking it completely apart. It is a lot easier to install all of the components with the case completely apart and everything out of the way. These are the basic steps:

1. Remove the main side panel (often these are easily removed simply by removing the thumbscrews).

2. Remove the back side panel (often these are easily removed simply by removing the thumbscrews).

3. Remove the front panel (bezel). Pull it from the bottom to detach from the spring-loaded tabs from the chassis frame.

4. Remove the power-supply unit (PSU) if one is included with your case. Use a screwdriver to remove the four screws holding the PSU to the rear of the chassis. Push the PSU forward and slide it out from the inside of the case.

5. Remove the rear chassis fan. Unclip it from the holding bracket and slide it out.

6. Remove the motherboard tray (if your case includes one). Remove the thumbscrew, press the latch and slide the tray forward, and then lift it up and out of the chassis.

7. Remove the front-panel port assembly (if your case in includes one). Remove one screw, and then pull the unit assembly forward and out of the case with the cables still attached.

8. Remove the front-panel switch/LED assembly. Unclip it from the front of the chassis and remove it with the cables attached.

Processor and Memory Installation

Now we are ready to install the motherboard. First we'll install the motherboard to the tray we previously removed from the chassis. We'll proceed by installing the processor, heatsink, and memory into the motherboard. If your chassis does not use a motherboard tray, you will need to lay your case on its side and install the motherboard directly in the case just as you would if you were installing the motherboard on a removable tray. The steps are as follows.

Install the Motherboard in the Tray

Make sure there are sufficient standoffs in the tray (or chassis) to support the board. There should be one standoff for each screw hole (metal plated hole) in the board. There are eight screw holes on this board, and eight standoffs in the tray. If necessary, add standoffs to the appropriate positions in the tray or chassis.

Mount the board on the removable tray, or inside the chassis if it does not have a removable tray. This particular tray uses no screws to mount the board. To mount it, set the board over the standoffs, slide the board slightly forward, and press down to lock the board in place.

Install the Processor in the Socket

1. Remove the protective cover plate from the processor socket.
2. Move the locking lever to the side, and then lift the lever to release the retaining cover plate.
3. Remove the protective cap from the bottom of the processor.
4. Set the processor in the socket, observing the proper orientation of the alignment notches.
5. Lower the cover plate, and then move the locking lever down until it clicks or locks into place. This puts pressure on the processor, ensuring good contact between the pads on the bottom of the processor and the pins in the socket.

Install the Heat Sink on the Processor

Thermal interface material (TIM) or thermal grease cannot be reused. New retail processors come with heat sinks that have preapplied TIM. If it is damaged, or if the heat sink has already been installed once, the existing TIM must be cleaned off and reapplied. Because I had already tested this processor in another system, I had to first clean off the old TIM, and apply new TIM from scratch. To do this, follow these steps:

1. Use a soft towel or cloth to remove the previous thermal grease from the heatsink and the top of the processor.
2. Apply new thermal grease to the top of the processor heat spreader (metal cap). Use the smallest amount that you can spread over the top of the chip, usually an amount the size of a BB is sufficient.
3. Use your finger (wearing a rubber glove to prevent contamination) or a hard-plastic card (such as a credit card) to spread the thermal grease in the thinnest possible layer covering the entire surface of the heat spreader (metal cap).
4. Make sure the heat sink locking pins are rotated in the proper position. The tops should be turned in the opposite direction of the arrows on top.
5. Set the heat sink on the processor such that the 4 pins engage in the holes surrounding the socket.
6. Push each of the 4 pins down until they click or latch into place. This can take more force than you might think is prudent.

7. Visually inspect to ensure that all 4 pins have fully engaged and are locked.

8. Plug in the 4-wire PWM (pulse width modulated) fan into the 4-wire CPU fan connector on the motherboard. The CPU fan connector should be near the processor socket.

9. Route the fan wire such that it won't interfere with the fan or any other components.

Install the Memory

Now we're ready to install the memory. In this system I am installing, the maximum amount recommended when running a 32-bit operating system is 3GB. This is because the system hardware uses most if not all of the fourth gigabyte of address space, meaning that if you install 4GB, you won't be able to use much more than 3GB anyway. If you need more than 3GB of RAM, you should install a 64-bit OS, which can use all the memory that the motherboard can support (8GB in this case).

To install the memory, follow these steps:

1. Organize the memory into matched pairs, which will be installed into different memory channels, allowing dual-channel operation. In this case, I have two 1GB modules, and two 512MB modules, for a total of 3GB of RAM.

2. Install the 1GB modules into the blue DIMM sockets, labeled DIMM 0, Channel A, and DIMM 0, Channel B. This will ensure that each is in a different channel, allowing dual-channel operation.

3. To physically install each module, first move the retaining tabs to the side, and then set the module over the socket such that the notch in the module aligns with the key in the socket. *Do not* install the module backward; both the module and the motherboard will be damaged if you power it on that way.

4. Continue by pressing down on the module until the locking tabs spring up and engage the retaining notches in the sides of the module. Ensure that the tabs are fully engaged and that the module is fully seated.

5. Repeat this procedure for the other modules.

6. Check to be sure all modules are fully seated and the locking tabs are fully engaged.

Motherboard Installation

Now we're ready to install the motherboard in the chassis. We'll start by installing the I/O shield in the chassis, and then install the motherboard into the chassis.

Note

Note that if your chassis does not include a motherboard tray, you would be installing the motherboard directly into the chassis in a manner similar to how we previously installed the motherboard into the tray.

1. Remove any existing I/O shield installed in the case.

2. Install the new I/O shield that came with your motherboard. Do this by setting the shield into place from the inside and snapping it into place.

3. Set the motherboard and tray assembly into the chassis. Ensure that all tabs are engaging, and then press down and slide the tray toward the rear of the chassis until the tray locks in place.

4. Inspect the installation to see that all tabs are fully engaged, and then install the thumb-screw to lock the tray and motherboard in place.

Drive Installation

Now we're ready to install the drives. I'm going to start from the top down and install the optical drive first, and then the hard disk drives. This system will not use a floppy drive, so we aren't going to install one. The chassis used in this video is tool-less, allowing for a very easy drive installation.

Optical Drive(s)

To install the optical drive, follow these steps:

1. Remove any EMI (electromagnetic interference) shield (if present).

2. Slide the locking mechanism backward to disengage the locking tabs.

3. Slide the drive in through the front of the chassis until the holes in the side of the drive are aligned with the locking tabs.

4. Slide the lock mechanism forward to engage the locking tabs which lock the drive in place.

Hard Drive(s)

To install the hard drives, follow these steps:

1. Pull the locking mechanisms on each side forward to disengage the locking tabs.

2. Slide the drive in through the side of the chassis until the holes in the side of the drive are aligned with the locking tabs.

3. Slide the locking mechanisms backward to engage the locking tabs, which locks the drive in place.

4. Repeat this for any other drive(s) you might have.

Front-Panel Connections

Now we're ready to make all the front-panel connections. I like to do this before any other cables are installed, because it makes it easier to see what you are doing, as these connections can be troublesome.

In the earlier section of this booklet, I described the many problems there can be with front-panel connections, and came up with solutions to those problems, too. What I did was to replace all the individual 1x1, 1x2, and 1x4 connectors (used to attach the front-panel ports and devices to the motherboard) with larger 2x5 connectors that make all the connections to each 2x5 header at once. This makes connecting the front-panel ports a breeze.

This particular chassis has the following front-panel connectors:

- Switch/LED
- Two dual-USB (4 ports total)
- Audio (microphone/headphone)
- FireWire

Because I changed the connector housings in advance, each of these is now a single 2x5 (10-pin) header connector rather than numerous smaller individual connectors. If your case uses the numerous tiny individual connectors, it will probably take you several times longer to install these connectors than what you see in the video. I highly recommend either purchasing cases that have 2x5 connectors or replacing your existing connectors with 2x5 housings.

To make the front-panel connections, I followed these steps:

1. Attach the front switch/LED assembly to the front of the chassis. It literally just snaps in place via preexisting holes and locking tabs.

2. Route the cable through the hole provided in the case.

3. Locate the 2x5 switch/LED header connector on the motherboard (it is usually multicolored), and plug the 2x5 connector housing in place, observing the proper orientation (the missing key pin in the header is pin 10). Note that although the header is keyed, the mating connector might not be keyed; so, ensure that it is in the proper orientation. Installing backward won't hurt anything in this case, but the switches and LEDs won't work properly unless they are plugged in correctly.

4. Mount the front-panel USB/audio/FireWire port assembly to the front of the chassis, while routing the cables through the provided hole. One screw locks the assembly in place.

5. Locate two free 2x5 dual-USB headers on the motherboard (this board has three of them), and plug in a 2x5 dual-USB connector into each of them. Motherboard USB headers are normally black in color. Ensure that they are plugged in with the proper orientation (the missing key pin in the header is pin 9), because damage can occur to the motherboard and any USB peripherals if they are connected backward.

6. Locate the 2x5 audio header on the motherboard, and plug in the 2x5 audio connector. Motherboard audio headers are normally yellow in color. Ensure that the connector is plugged in with the proper orientation (the missing key pin in the header is pin 8).

7. Locate the 2x5 FireWire header on the motherboard, and plug in the 2x5 FireWire connector. Motherboard FireWire headers are normally blue (1394a) or red (1394b). Ensure that the connector is plugged in with the proper orientation (the missing key pin in the header is pin 9).

8. Route the cables away from other components.

Cooling Fans and Power-Supply Installation

Now we're ready to install the cooling fans and power supply. I like to install the fans first because it is a lot easier with the power supply out of the way. This case came with a 92mm rear fan, and has a space for an optional 80mm front fan, which I am adding during the installation. In many cases, I like to replace all the fans in a chassis with quieter fans that use fluid bearings.

Fan Installation

To install the fans, I followed these steps:

1. Observe the directional arrows on the fan indicating both blade rotation and airflow.

2. Install the rear fan such that the arrow (and airflow) is out the rear of the case. In this chassis, the fan just snaps into a preinstalled bracket.

3. Connect the fan power plug to the rear chassis fan connector on the motherboard.

4. To install the front fan, temporarily remove the front-panel switch/LED assembly, and then remove the fan retaining plate (thumbscrew).

5. Install the front fan such that the arrow (and airflow) is directed into the case.

6. Set the fan into the receptacle while routing the cable through, and then set the retaining plate in place and reattach the thumbscrew.

7. Reattach the switch/LED assembly.

8. Connect the front fan plug to the front (or auxiliary) fan connector on the motherboard.

Power-Supply Installation

To install the power supply, first note all the connectors on the supply, and figure out which ones will be necessary and where they will go. In particular, you have the 24-pin and 4-pin motherboard power connectors, SATA power connectors, and standard peripheral (sometimes called Molex) power connectors. If you don't have enough SATA connectors, you can get adapters.

1. Slide the power supply into the chassis from the inside.

2. Attach the 4 mounting screws from the rear.

3. Connect the motherboard power connectors, both the main and +12V (CPU power) connectors.

4. Connect the drive power connectors to the optical and hard disk drives. Some will use SATA power connectors, whereas others will use the standard peripheral (Molex) type.

Drive Cables

Now we're ready to connect the SATA cables between the motherboard and the drives. In this build, I am using a SATA optical drive and two SATA HDDs. To attach them, I followed these steps:

1. Locate the SATA ports on the motherboard, and determine the port numbering and position so that you know which is port 0, 1, 2, and so on.

2. Connect a SATA cable between the first hard disk drive and port 0.

3. Connect a SATA cable between the second hard disk drive and port 1, and then repeat until all hard drives are connected.

4. Connect a cable between the next available SATA port and the optical drive.

5. If using PATA (Parallel ATA) optical drive, ensure the drive is jumpered to CS (Cable Select) and connect an 80-conductor PATA ribbon cable between the PATA port on the motherboard and the drive. In that case, the blue cable connector should go to the motherboard, while the black connector goes to the drive.

Finish Up the System

At this point, the system is technically ready to run! However, I don't consider it truly finished until I spend some time "dressing" the cables, which means rerouting them for the cleanest possible installation. I consider fully dressed cables the hallmark of a professional system builder, and likewise consider a "rat's nest" of jumbled wires the sure sign of an amateur.

I like to route the cables such that the motherboard is fully uncovered, uncluttered, and exposed, and maximum airflow is allowed throughout the chassis. Where possible, I route cables along the edges of the chassis, and tie them up with nylon zip ties to keep them in place.

Look at the difference in the system between when it was technically finished and when the cables were all fully "dressed" and you'll see what I mean. In the end, dressing the cables doesn't really require any technical skill, just some common sense, patience, and a few zip ties.

After the cables have been fully dressed, you can reattach the back side panel, front panel, and main side panel. When attaching the main side panel, if it contains a CAG or processor duct, you'll want to set the depth of the duct such that it ends up between 12mm and 20mm from the top of the processor fan. This will allow maximum airflow to the processor.

At that point, the system is truly finished and ready to run!

Video Segment 5: System Startup

At this point, we're ready to power on the system for the first time. To prepare for this, I've connected the following:

- Keyboard
- Mouse

- Display

- Power

Note that I have not yet connected a network cable. I usually like to do that after the OS has been installed, along with any service packs, and after I ensure that the built-in firewall is turned on.

Power On, Enter BIOS Setup

To get the system running, I followed these steps:

1. Power the system on, observe the display until you see the prompt to enter the BIOS Setup, which is F2 in this system.

2. Press the appropriate key (F2) when prompted. You should now be in the BIOS setup. If you didn't press the key in time, reset the system and try again. (Depending on the BIOS you are running, you might need to press Esc or another key to enter your BIOS setup program.)

3. Check the BIOS version reported on the main setup screen; ensure that it is the latest version. If not, now would be a good time to install the updated Flash BIOS image. The easiest method to do a BIOS upgrade on newer systems is via a bootable CD containing the BIOS image. To do this, on another system visit the motherboard manufacturer website and download the bootable CD image (*.iso) file. Burn this image to a CD, and then place the CD into the optical drive of the new system and reset it. Follow the prompts on the screen to complete the BIOS update.

Note

Many motherboards will not support bootable CD BIOS upgrades via SATA optical drives. In that situation, you need to temporarily install a PATA optical drive to complete the upgrade, or perform the upgrade via one of the other available procedures such as via a Windows-based executable or a bootable USB Flash drive.

4. Check the various BIOS setup screens to ensure that your processor and memory are being properly recognized and supported. Check CPU type, speed, cache, total RAM, dual-channel mode, and so on.

5. Disable any ports or devices that will not be used, such as serial ports, parallel ports, consumer infrared ports, and so forth.

6. Check the drive configuration; ensure that the system is set to AHCI (Advanced Host Controller Interface) at a minimum, or even better, ensure that it is set to RAID (Redundant Array of Independent Disks) mode. I recommend RAID mode even if you don't plan on using RAID, because it includes all AHCI functionality and allows for a future RAID migration without having to reinstall the OS or drivers. This is called "RAID Ready." Set to IDE (backward-compatible) mode if you are installing an older OS that does not have AHCI or RAID drivers. This will unfortunately reduce driver performance because advanced SATA features such as NCQ (Native Command Queuing) will be disabled.

7. Check to see that all the installed drives are being detected.

8. Check fan control and hardware monitoring to see that all fans are being recognized and that the fans are reporting proper rotational speeds. Also observe component temperatures. Note that some components such as the chipset ICH (I/O controller hub) are "designed" to run at up to from 90 to 115°C (up to 239°F), so high temperatures are normal and even expected for that chip.

9. Check memory configuration. I recommend leaving the default auto settings, which will automatically set the memory timing according to the modules you have installed.

10. Check the chipset configuration. If running Windows Vista, I recommend enabling the HPET (High Precision Event Timer); it is supported in Vista but not in Windows XP.

11. In the Security menu, enable VT (Virtualization Technology). This allows virtualization software such as Virtual PC or VMware to use the hardware virtualization circuitry in the chip, which improves the performance of virtualized operating systems and applications.

12. In the Power menu, check the ACPI Suspend State, ensure that it is set to S3 (Suspend to RAM) rather than S1 (sleep), because S3 uses virtually the same amount of power as being completely off, saving up to $100 per year or more in energy costs *per system*!

13. In the Boot menu, check the boot order; ensure that the bootable optical drive precedes the hard disks, which will enable a successful OS installation from CD or DVD.

14. Exit, saving changes.

Install the Operating System

At this point, you are ready to install the OS on your newly built machine. Installing the OS is not covered in this video, but it is covered in the DVD included with my book *Upgrading and Repairing Windows*. I will also be producing a standalone DVD that covers installing Windows in the future.

Although there isn't time to cover a full Windows installation on the DVD, I can give you some tips. If you are installing Windows Vista, the installation is very simple. You won't need any special drivers even if you have the SATA controller set to AHCI or RAID mode as I demonstrated in the video. You merely insert the disc, and follow the prompts to install Vista. If you want to install Vista on an array, before the installation process starts, reset the system and press Ctrl+I when prompted. This invokes the BIOS-based Intel Matrix RAID manager, which enables you to configure an array even before you install an OS. Note that you won't be prompted for Ctrl+I unless you have the system in a "RAID Ready" configuration (SATA controller in RAID mode) and you have at least two hard drives installed.

You'll find that the Intel Matrix RAID configuration is extremely easy; and, after you exit, you can boot from the Vista DVD and install to a RAID volume just as easily as a single drive. One caveat: I did notice that if I created multiple RAID volumes in a single array (possible with the Intel RAID controller), Vista gets confused and won't recognize the volumes. The solution was to create only a single volume, install Vista on that, and then after Vista was installed I could create the second volume, which I was using for data storage.

Installing Windows XP is a whole other matter. Because XP does not have the AHCI/RAID drivers integrated into the install disc by default (even with SP3), you have to use either the F6 driver install method or manually integrate the drivers into a custom-made XP install disc. Because the motherboard I used in this video didn't have a floppy controller, and because the F6 procedure doesn't work with USB floppy drives (technically it does, but only with three specific rare models that have long been discontinued), you have to use the integration method. Although this can be done manually following detailed instructions on the Intel site, I recommend taking the easy way out and using the BTS Driverpacks to create a custom XP install disc with their MassStorage Driverpack fully integrated. For more information, see http://www.driverpacks.net.

In addition to the MassStorage Driverpack, I also recommend integrating the Chipset Driverpack because I was unable to get the chipset drivers properly installed in Windows XP otherwise, without having them shut down the USB controllers, which rendered my keyboard and mouse non-functional. Because this motherboard doesn't include standard PS/2 keyboard and mouse ports, I couldn't take control of the system to repair the problem (USB was disabled even in Safe mode), forcing me to reinstall from scratch. Fortunately, integrating the chipset drives into the installation CD solved that problem with XP. Note that these problems wouldn't be much of an issue on other 3x series chipset-based motherboards that have both a floppy controller and standard PS/2 keyboard/mouse ports.

After you have the OS installed, I recommend installing the drivers next, and then any service packs (that weren't already integrated into the OS install disc), and finally any OS updates. For that last step, you need to connect the network cable and go online, but by that time you should have at least XP with SP2 installed, and that or any newer OS (including Vista) will have the built-in firewall turned on by default.

After the OS updates, you can install your favorite applications and put the system in service.

Conclusion

Well, that concludes this video and booklet! Thanks for watching, and I surely hope you find the information both in the video and in this booklet useful and informative. Please visit my forum at http://forum.scottmueller.com if you have any questions or comments. Thanks again, Scott.